THE (no sugar) DELICIOUS DESSERT COOKBOOK

Jeanne Moe, R.D.
Karen Rubin, R.D.
Sally Abrams, R.D.

Celestial Arts
Berkeley, California

Copyright 1984
by Celestial Arts
P.O. Box 7327
Berkeley, California 94707

No part of this book may be reproduced by any mechanical photographic or electronic process, or in the form of a phonographic recording, nor may it be stored in a retrieval system, transmitted, or otherwise copied for public or private use without the written permission of the publisher.

Cover design: Kim Gale
Interior design: Kim Gale
Composition: Lewis Publishing

Made in the United States of America

Library of Congress Catalog Card no. 84-70860
ISBN 0-89087-402-6

DEDICATION

This book is dedicated with love to Rick and Erik Moe, Russ Rubin, and Michael and Leigh Abrams.

ACKNOWLEDGMENTS

We wish to thank Linda Roghaar for her invaluable assistance in every aspect of this cookbook, from conception to publication. Without her advice and moral support this book would never have materialized.

We also wish to thank G. D. Searle & Co. for their cooperation in allowing us to use EQUAL® Tabletop Sweetener in our recipe.

The Exchange information in the Appendix is from *The Elegant Touch Cookbook*. We thank authors Marjorie Zats and Karen Rubin for their permission to include the exchanges in this book.

"EQUAL® is a registered trademark of G. D. Searle & Co. and is used herein with its permission. The recipes in this book have been prepared by the authors. G. D. Searle & Co. has neither endorsed nor approved these recipes."

CONTENTS

About The Authors viii
Introduction ix
What Is Aspartame? x
About Our Recipes 1
How To Use This Book 3

An asterisk following the recipe designates particularly low cholesterol, saturated fats and sodium.

COOKIES AND SNACKS 4
   No-Bake Chocolate Cookies* 6
   Chocolate Rum Bonbons 6
   Cocoa-Coconut Balls* 7
   Cranberry Crisp* 8
   Date Squares 8
   Lemon Morsels* 9
   Orange Kisses* 10
   Peanut Butter Balls* 10
   Raisin Applesauce Squares 11
   Rhubarb Crisp* 12
   Slippery Squares* 13

PUDDINGS, MOUSSES AND SOUFFLES 14
   Amaretto Souffle 16
   Apricot Souffle 17
   Chocolate Mousse 18
   Chocolate Pudding* 19
   Custard 20
   Instant Orange Mousse* 21
   Mocha Chiffon 22
   Pineapple Cheese Dream 23
   Pumpkin Pudding* 24
   Raisin Rice Pudding* 25
   Raspberry Yogurt Sublime 26
   Tapioca Pudding 27
   Vanilla Pudding 28
   Lemon Pudding* 29

SAUCES, TOPPINGS, AND FILLINGS 10
- Brandied Blackberry Sauce* 32
- Vanilla Cream Sauce or Filling 32
- Strawberry Topping* 33
- Pineapple Sauce or Filling 34
- Lemon Sauce* 34
- Buttered Rum Sauce 35
- Granola Topping* 36
- Fudge Sauce* 37
- Custard Sauce* 38
- Cranberry Sauce* 38
- Cranberry Orange Relish* 39
- Coconut Cream Sauce Or Filling* 40
- Chocolate Cream Sauce Or Filling* 40
- Cherry Rum Sauce* 41

FRUIT DESSERTS 42
- Apricot Fruit Compote* 43
- Cinnamon Glazed Pineapple* 44
- Fruit Pie* 45
- Apple Crisp* 46
- Pears in Custard 47
- Saucy Rhubarb* 48
- Strawberry Rhubarb Compote* 48
- Tutti Fruitty Dessert 49

FROZEN DESSERTS 50
- Apple Sorbet* 51
- Blueberry Ice* 52
- Cherry Yogurt Freeze* 52
- Double-Layer Chocolate Freeze 53
- Citrus Frozen Desserts* 54
- Cranberry Sorbet* 54
- Frozen Espresso* 55
- Frozen Lemon Dessert 56
- Fruit And Yogurt Sherbet* 56
- Lemon Sherbet* 57
- Mint Sherbet* 58
- Mixed Fruit Ice* 59
- Mocha Treat 60
- Vanilla Air* 61

PIES	62
Apple Graham Pie*	64
Banana Bavarian Pie*	65
Banana Cream Pie	66
Black Bottom Pie*	67
Blizzard Pie	68
Blueberry Tarts*	69
Chocolate Eggnog Pie	70
Cranberry Chiffon Pie	71
Dreamy Chocolate Pie	72
Eggnog Pie	73
Fresh Peach Pie*	74
Lemon Chiffon Pie*	75
Refrigerator Pumpkin Pie	76
Rum Chiffon Pie	77
Strawberry Bavarian Pie	78
Chocolate Crumb Crust*	79
Chocolate Wafer Crust*	79
Graham Cracker Crust*	80
Pastry Crust	81
DRINKABLE DESSERTS	82
Banana Shake*	83
Cafe Au Lait*	84
Cappuccino	84
Chocolate Nog	85
Citrus Buttermilk Cooler*	85
Cocoa*	86
Cranberry Juice*	86
New Year's Eggnog	87
Fruit Frappe*	88
Frozen Fruit Slush	89
Grasshopper Shake*	89
Hot Chocolate Excelsior	90
Hot Cider*	90
Hot Spiced Tea*	91
Lemonade*	91
Orange Juliet*	92
Rhubarb Punch*	92
Winter Warmer	93

GELATINS 94
- Blackberry Gelatin Mold* 96
- Cranberries And Cream Gelatin Mold* 96
- Fruit Cocktail Gelatin* 97
- Raspberry Bavarian* 98
- Sugar-Free Gelatin* 98
- Zero-Calorie Cranberry Gelatin* 99

ELEGANT DESSERTS 100
- Blueberry Angel Cake 101
- Cheeseberry Crepes 102
- Dessert Crepes 103
- Eclaires 104
- Lemon Cheesecake 105
- Peach Charlotte* 106
- Spanish Cream With Strawberry Sauce 107
- Trifle 108

APPENDIX: Exchange Information   109

About the Authors

Jeanne Moe is a registered dietitian who received her B.S. in foods and nutrition from Mankato State University and completed a dietetic internship at Howard University Hospitals, Washington, D.C. She has worked as a nutrition educator in a variety of health facilities and presently specializes in the area of weight control and diabetes. Ms. Moe contributed to *The Elegant Touch Cookbook* and *Microwaving on a Diet*. She has spoken to numerous groups on health, sports nutrition, and child nutrition.

Karen Rubin is a registered dietitian. She received her B.S. in nutrition and dietetics from the University of Minnesota and completed her dietetic internship at Beth Israel Hospital in Boston. In her twelve years as a nutrition educator, Karen has worked in a broad range of community and hospital settings. She has developed and taught a variety of community courses, ranging from low-calorie cooking and cardiac nutrition to nutrition and wellness. Ms. Rubin is the coauthor of *The Elegant Touch Cookbook* for dieters and diabetics and contributed to *Microwaving on a Diet*, part of the Microwave Library series.

Sally Abrams is a registered dietitian who completed her B.S. and internship in dietetics at the University of Minnesota. She has worked as a nutritionist in the health care field with an emphasis on diabetes education. She is currently working as a consultant in a physicians' clinic specializing in the area of weight control and behavioral change. Ms. Abrams has taught classes in nutrition for pregnant women, nutrition for marathon runners, and other topics.

Introduction

Can't I have dessert? Must the answer be no?

One of the toughest parts of our jobs as professional nutritionists has been to recommend appropriate desserts for people who need to limit sugar, fat, and calories. Although many dieters may be willing to cut out big meals and eat smaller portions, few people will eliminate desserts forever. It's just too much of a sacrifice, and the choice have been too limited. How long can you be satisfied with just fresh fruit or a one-inch slice of angel food cake for dessert? When we included a truly delicious dessert in a diet plan, the portion could have been served in a thimble! Like many nutritionists, we were frustrated because we could recommend so few desserts that were satisfying, yet low in calories.

A new low-calorie sweetener, aspartame, ended this frustration. We could at last develop recipes for delicious desserts that are good for you. Aspartame tastes remarkably like sugar but has a mere fraction of the calories. It is made from protein, a safe and natural food. Unlike saccharin, it does not leave a bitter or metallic aftertaste.

To create a truly healthful dessert, it is not enough to just eliminate sugar and sweeten with aspartame. We have gone a step further by reducing fats and cholesterol. Through extensive testing, tasting, and retesting we have come up with desserts that everyone — family and friends, dieters and non-dieters alike—can enjoy.

Here's to happy eating and healthy living!

Jeanne Moe
Karen Rubin
Sally Abrams

What Is Aspartame?

The discovery of aspartame was a lucky accident. In 1965 a chemist, James Schlatter, was busy in his laboratory. During the course of his work, he licked his finger to pick up a piece of paper and noticed an incredibly sweet taste. He discovered that by combining the amino acids phenylalanine and aspartic acid, he had created a very sweet-tasting compound. Thus, aspartame was born. Years of research followed to assure aspartame's safety, and in 1981 aspartame was approved for consumer use. Soon after, it began appearing on grocery store shelves under the trademark Nutrasweet and as an ingredient of the sweetener Equal®. (Equal® is a registered trademark of G. D. Searle & Co.)

Unlike other sweeteners, aspartame is totally natural, treated by the body like any other protein. Aspartame tastes remarkably like sugar and leaves no bitter or metallic aftertaste. Because aspartame is approximately 200 times sweeter than sugar, only tiny amounts are needed to make foods sweet. In fact, aspartame is so concentrated that it had to be mixed with dextrose powder to create a product with enough volume to be measured.

Even with the few calories in the dextrose, aspartame sweeteners have substantially fewer calories than equal amounts of sugar. For instance, one packet of aspartame is equal in sweetness to two teaspoons of sugar. The aspartame contains only 4 calories while the sugar contains 32. Aspartame's great taste and negligible calories make it ideal for everyone, especially dieters and others who need to limit their intake of sweets. It is even sodium free, unlike saccharin.

Aspartame is extremely versatile. You can use it in many different desserts, as you will discover when you leaf through this book. Although aspartame works well in many recipes, you generally cannot use it in desserts that require long baking in a conventional oven. However, we have had success with recipes baked in the microwave oven! Because aspartame does not provide the necessary volume and structure, it will not work when substituted for sugar in cakes, breads, and some baked goods.

At the present, aspartame is available only in single-serving packets. In the future, it may be available in bulk. For that reason, we list both the number of packets and the weight in grams needed in our recipes. Aspartame intensifies the natural sweetness of fruits, so fewer packets are used in fruit desserts. On the other hand, chocolate requires proportionally more aspartame to achieve a sweet taste.

About Our Recipes

Our recipes are unique.
* No recipe calls for sugar.
  * All but a few of our desserts are below 200 calories per serving. Many deserts are even below 100 calories!
* We have reduced cholesterol and saturated fats to the lowest possible level without sacrificing taste.
* The Dietary Guideline, a result of the goals developed by the U.S. Senate, has guided our philosophy in developing these recipes. Here are the highlights of the guidelines with specific examples from our recipes.

1. Eat a variety of foods.
Our desserts contain a variety of nutritious foods, including fruits, dairy products, grains, and protein. These add to the variety and interest of the meal. Our desserts also vary in texture and flavor, which help enhance a well-balanced meal.

2. Maintain ideal weight.
Maintaining your ideal body weight is a key part of staying healthy. Whether you are already at the right weight or struggling to get there, our desserts can help you. They provide a satisfying end to your meal without the excessive calories of most desserts. They have been developed to save you calories. Just look at a few examples:

Recipe	Calories per Serving in Original	Calories Per Serving in Our Serving
Banana Cream Pie	353	197
Chocolate Mousse	379	130
Fudge Sauce	91	16

You can enjoy our desserts with a clear conscience. They are low enough in calories to fit into anyone's diet!

3. Avoid too much fat, saturated fat, and cholesterol.

Excessive fat is a real culprit in the American diet. Too much of the wrong kind of fat (cholesterol and saturated fat) can lead to heart disease, cancer, and obesity. The recipes in our cookbook call for the right kind of fats (polyunsaturated) whenever possible without sacrificing consistency and taste. We have also limited the total amount of fat. Of course, limiting fat also limits saturated fat and cholesterol. Reducing fat greatly reduces total calories as well.

One example is Banana Bavarian Pie, which contains no cholesterol. This dessert would normally have whipped cream, but we use evaporated or powdered skim milk instead. Evaporated skim milk is an excellent source of protein, calcium, and vitamin A, yet it is low in calories and contains no fat. Many of our recipes, such as Amaretto Souffle and Peach Charlotte, call for egg whites rather than whole eggs because egg yolks are high in cholesterol. This way, we can still achieve the desired consistency and taste without cholesterol or fat.

4. Eat foods with adequate starch and fiber.

The value of starches and fiber in the diet is well-known. In addition to fiber's health benefits, high-fiber foods are the calorie counter's friend. High-fiber foods are low in calories and satisfyingly filling. Fruits and whole grains, are excellent sources of fiber and appear frequently in our recipes. For example, check out Fruit Pie, Granola Topping, and Date Squares for some tasty high-fiber fare!

5. Avoid too much sugar.

These desserts eliminate processed sugars completely yet retain a sweet taste. Processed sugars provide "empty" calories and very little else. Just two tablespoons of sugar per day is equal to 35,000 calories per year, or ten pounds of body fat. Our sugarless creations save you hundreds of calories per serving. We were able to remove over 1000 calories in our Eggnog Pie by eliminating sugar and using aspartame.

6. Avoid too much sodium.

Homemade desserts are not traditionally a source of excess sodium. As you leaf through this cookbook, you will notice that a few of our recipes call for salt, but usually just a "pinch." This pinch of salt enhances sweetness. Our desserts are much lower in sodium than frozen or prepackaged desserts that include sodium-containing preservatives. Our desserts are lower in sodium than those made with saccharin because saccharin contains sodium and aspartame does not!

7. If you drink alcoholic beverages, do so in moderation.

How to Use This Book

To help you make the most of our recipes, we include the following information:

Calories: Calories per serving are listed. We think our servings are generous, but remember, even our desserts are high calorie if you eat six or eight servings!

Food Exchange: For those planning meals according to the food exchanges developed by the American Diabetes and Dietetic Associations, we list the exchanges per serving in all of our recipes. For information on the exchange lists, please see the Appendix, page 109.

♡ :A heart symbol designates recipes that are particularly low in cholesterol, saturated fats, and sodium.

Microwave: A few of our desserts require cooking in a microwave oven. All such are clearly designated. The majority of our desserts use conventional cooking methods but can be adapted to the microwave easily.

Hints: At the beginning of each chapter we include hints to help you prepare the desserts in that section. Please read the hints carefully to get the best results.

Garnishes and Serving Suggestions: We suggest ways to garnish and serve your desserts so they will be as pleasing to the eye as they are to the palate. The garnishes are optional and are not calculated in the exchanges given per serving. Maintain portion control. If you load down your desserts with excessive garnish, you will substantially increase the calories.

HINTS TO MAKE YOUR COOKIES AND SNACKS A SUCCESS

Are you looking for a low-calorie morsel to satisfy your urge to snack? The recipes in this chapter will satisfy the cookie monster in you. These snacks and cookies make terrific lunch-bag treats, hostess gifts, and coffee break goodies.

Store each recipe separately in an airtight container.

These treats pack easily and keep well if wrapped in plastic sandwich bags. Add them to bag lunches for a special surprise.

If you are making your own graham cracker crumbs, use 12 (2-inch) squares for 1 cup of crushed crumbs.

A food processor works wonders for crushing crackers, wafers, and zweiback. A food processor is not absolutely necessary, though. You can crush with a rolling pin: break up the crackers, put them in a plastic bag, press out the air, seal up, and roll.

CHOCOLATE GELATIN SQUARES

4 envelopes (4 Tbsp.) unflavored gelatin
1½ cups cold water
12 Packets (12 grams) EQUAL® Tabletop Sweetener
1 package (12 oz.) semisweet chocolate chips

Mix gelatin and water in a medium saucepan. Let stand 1 minute. Stir over low heat until gelatin is completely dissolved, about 5 minutes. Add chocolate and continue cooking, stirring constantly, until chocolate is melted. Take off heat and add 12 packets Equal. With wire whip or rotary beater, beat mixture until chocolate is blended. Pour into an 8- or 9-inch baking pan; cool to room temperature, then refrigerate.

If you have a craving for chocolate, three squares may satisfy the urge!

Yield: 72 (1-inch) squares
Exchanges: 1 Fruit and 1 Fat per 3 squares
Calories: 73 per 3 squares

NO-BAKE CHOCOLATE COOKIES ♡

24 packets (24 grams) EQUAL® Tabletop Sweetener
¼ cup margarine
½ cup skim milk
2 Tbsp. cocoa powder
½ cup peanut butter
2½ cups rolled oats
½ tsp. vanilla extract

Place margarine, milk, and cocoa together in a two-quart saucepan. Heat until the liquid boils, stirring continuously. Remove from heat and stir in peanut butter, Equal, and oats. Stir in vanilla. Drop by teaspoonfuls onto waxed paper. Cool in freezer.

Fill up your cookie jar with these easy-to-fix chocolate treats.

Yield: 50 cookies
Exchanges: 1 Fat and 1 Fruit per 2 cookies
Calories: 80

CHOCOLATE RUM BONBONS

1½ squares (1½ oz.) unsweetened baking chocolate
½ cup evaporated skim milk
½ tsp. rum extract
6 packets (6 grams) EQUAL® Tabletop Sweetener
1½ cups graham cracker crumbs or 8 (2-inch) squares, crushed
½ cup unsweetened coconut, finely shredded

Melt chocolate in double boiler over medium heat. Stir in milk and rum extract, mix well. Add graham cracker crumbs and Equal, mix well, and remove from heat. Chill until dough is cool and easy to handle. Roll into 3 large balls, then divide each ball into 12 pieces. Using the palms of your hands, roll each piece into a small ball. Chop the shredded coconut finely, then roll each ball in chopped coconut. Place on tray lined with waxed paper and refrigerate until ready to serve.

These bonbons are very attractive served in individual candy papers and arranged on a fancy candy plate.

Yield: 36 bonbons
Exchanges: 1 Fruit per 2 bonbons
Calories: 52

COCOA-COCONUT BALLS ♡

4 zwieback rounds
1 tsp. cocoa powder
2 Tbsp. water
4 packets (4 grams) EQUAL® Tabletop Sweetener
1 Tbsp. unsweetened coconut, very finely chopped

Crush zwieback until very fine (a food processor works well for this). Mix cocoa and water, then add zwieback and remaining ingredients. Divide mixture into 4 parts. Divide each part into 5 pieces (approximately ½ tablespoon each). Roll each piece into a ball.

Complement these chewy, chocolate treats with a hot cup of Cappuccino (page 84).

Yield: 20 cookies
Exchanges: 2 cookies FREE 1 Fruit per 5 cookies
Calories: 16 per 2 cookies
40 per 5 cookies

COOKIES AND SNACKS

CRANBERRY CRISP ♡

    2 cups (½ lb.) cranberries, fresh or frozen
    ⅓ cup water
    20 packets (20 grams) EQUAL® Tabletop Sweetener
    ½ cup quick-cooking rolled oats
    ¼ cup flour
    ¼ cup margarine

Combine cranberries, water, and Equal in a 9-inch ovenware pie dish. Cover with waxed paper and cook in microwave on high setting for 2½ to 3½ minutes, or until cranberries are tender. Combine oats and flour, cut in margarine until crumbly, and sprinkle over cranberry mixture. Cook for 6 to 7 minutes, or until crisp mixture is bubbling.

Frozen cranberries are available year-round, so you can enjoy Cranberry Crisp anytime. If your grocer does not stock frozen cranberries, purchase them in the fall and freeze them right in the bag.

                                           Servings: 5
                    Exchanges: 1 Bread and 2 Fats
                                       Calories: 183

DATE SQUARES

    ¾ cup chopped dates
    2 Tbsp. margarine
    1 egg
    1 Tbsp. skim milk
    1 tsp. vanilla extract
    ½ tsp. salt
    4 packets (4 grams) EQUAL® Tabletop Sweetener
    3 cups toasted rice cereal
    ¼ cup unsweetened coconut, chopped

Mix chopped dates, margarine, egg, milk, vanilla, and salt in a medium saucepan. Place over medium heat about 5 minutes until mixture is thick. Cool, then stir in Equal, then cereal. For bars, press mixture into a 9-inch non-stick pan. Sprinkle with coconut and refrigerate until firm. Cut into 24 bars. For fancy cookies, roll the mixture into 24 balls, then roll each ball in coconut. It will take an additional ½ cup coconut to do this.

Date squares are low in calories and nutritious. What more could you ask?

Yield: 24 bars or cookies
Exchanges: 1 Fruit
Calories: 39 per bar
44 per cookie

LEMON MORSELS ♡

36 vanilla wafers
3 Tbsp. lemon juice
¼ tsp. lemon extract
4 packets (4 grams) EQUAL® Tabletop Sweetener

Crush wafers until very fine (a food processor works well for this). Mix the wafer crumbs with the lemon juice, lemon extract, and Equal. Divide mixture into 4 parts. Divide each part into 7 pieces. Roll each piece into a ball.

Lemon Morsels are a delicate refreshment for a bridal shower, tea, or bridge club meeting.

Yield: 28 cookies
Exchanges: ½ Fruit per 2 cookies
Calories: 22 per cookie

ORANGE KISSES ♡

    36 vanilla wafers
    2 Tbsp. orange juice concentrate
    2 packets (2 grams) EQUAL® Tabletop Sweetener
    2 Tbsp. unsweetened coconut, very finely chopped

    Crush wafers until very fine (a food processor works well for this). Mix the wafer crumbs with orange juice concentrate, Equal, and coconut. Divide mixture into 4 parts. Divide each part into 5 pieces (approximately ½ tablespoon each). Roll each piece into a ball.

These are a sure hit with those who crave the tangy taste of citrus.

Yield: 28 cookies
Exchanges: 1 Fruit per 2 cookies)
Calories: 42 per 2 cookies

PEANUT BUTTER BALLS ♡

    36 vanilla wafers
    2 Tbsp. peanut butter
    2 Tbsp. water
    2 Tbsp. peanuts, finely chopped
    4 packets (4 grams) EQUAL® Tabletop Sweetener

    Crush wafers until very fine (a food processor works well for this). Mix the peanut butter with the water. Add the vanilla wafers, Equal, and chopped peanuts. Divide mixture into 4 parts. Divide each part into 7 pieces (approximately ½ tablespoon each). Roll each piece into a ball.

These are a versatile treat. When served in tiny paper or foil cups, they are pretty party fare for adults. Roll into fun forms—balls squares, and cones—to captivate kids at a birthday party.

Yield: 28 cookies
Exchanges: ½ Fat and ½ Fruit per 2 cookies
Calories: 45 per 2 cookies

RAISIN APPLESAUCE SQUARES

Microwave only

½ cup margarine
10 packets (10 grams) EQUAL® Tabletop Sweetener
¼ cup applesauce
1 cup sifted all-purpose flour
1 tsp. baking powder
¼ tsp. cinnamon
1 egg
1 tsp. vanilla extract
½ tsp. maple flavoring
¼ cup raisins

Place a small glass mixing bowl with the margarine into the microwave. Cook on medium high setting (70 percent power) for 1 minute. Stir Equal and applesauce into the margarine. Sift together flour, baking powder, and cinnamon. Stir into margarine mixture. Beat in egg. Stir in vanilla extract and maple flavoring. Spread mixture in an 8-inch glass baking dish. Sprinkle raisins on top. Cook, uncovered, on high setting for 4 minutes. Turn the dish and continue cooking on high setting for 1 to 1½ minutes, or until set. Cut into 16 squares. Bring to room temperature.

Serve with Hot Spiced Tea (page 91) for a crisp autumn treat.

Yield: 16 squares
Exchanges: ½ Bread and ½ Fat per 1 square
1 Bread and 1 Fat per 2 squares
Calories: 51 per square

RHUBARB CRISP ♡

*microwave only

2 cups rhubarb, diced
2 Tbsp. lemon juice
12 packets (12 grams) EQUAL® Tabletop Sweetener
grated rind of ½ a lemon
¾ cup flour
¼ cup rolled oats
¼ cup soft margarine

Dice cleaned rhubarb into ½-inch pieces. Add lemon juice and Equal. Mix well. Spread in bottom of a square 8-inch glass baking dish and sprinkle lemon rind on top. Combine flour, rolled oats, and margarine. Mix together until crumbly. Sprinkle on top of rhubarb. Microwave on high setting, uncovered, 15 minutes, turning dish 3 times. Let stand 5 minutes. Serve hot or at room temperature.

This crisp is pleasant both winter or summer. For frozen rhubarb, use a little more than 2 cups; microwave 1 minute on high setting, drain, then follow recipe above.

Servings: 16
Exchanges: ½ Bread and 1 Fat
Calories: 80

SLIPPERY SQUARES ♡

4 envelopes (4 Tbsp.) unflavored gelatin
3 cups unsweetened fruit juice, divided
3 packets (3 grams) EQUAL® Tabletop Sweetener

Combine 1½ cup juice with gelatin in a medium saucepan. Heat until gelatin is completely dissolved. Remove from heat, stir in

COOKIES AND SNACKS 13

remaining cold juice and Equal. Pour into an 8-inch baking pan and chill until firm. To serve, cut into 2-inch squares.

These squares are easy to make. Use any fresh, canned, or prepared frozen unsweetened juice except fresh or frozen pineapple juice.

Yield: 16 squares
2 squares = 1 fruit (if orange or grapefruit juice is used)
1 square = 1 fruit (if other juices are used)
Calories: 42 per square if orange or grapefruit juice is used
32-42 per 1 square if other juices are used

HINTS TO MAKE YOUR PUDDINGS, MOUSSES, AND SOUFFLES A SUCCESS

Both family and friends will be delighted when you serve these low-calorie versions of popular favorites. From old-fashioned Rice Pudding to elegant Chocolate Mousse, this chapter has recipes to please everyone. End your meal tonight with one of these smooth, creamy desserts.

To make the most of EQUAL® Table Sweetener's flavor, be sure you add it after removing your heated mixture from the stove. Likewise, to preserve the flavor of flavorings and extracts, add them after stovetop cooking is completed.

Look for Neufchatel cheese (pronounced NEW-shatell) next to the cream cheese in the dairy case at your grocery store. Similar in flavor and texture to cream cheese but lower in fat and calories, Neufchatel is a real find. If this is not available look for low calorie cream cheese.

Cover your finished puddings with a layer of plastic wrap to prevent a skin from forming.

Here are a few hints to help you prepare the egg whites called for in some of these recipes.

- If you have difficulty separating eggs, use a small funnel. Carefully crack the egg into the funnel, and the white should slip through the funnel into a bowl below.
- Never throw away leftover egg whites. Simply pour them into a plastic freezer container, label, and date. Or you may pour whites into ice cream trays (1 egg white per section). When they are frozen, pop them out and store them in plastic bags After you thaw them, you can use them just like fresh whites. If you wish, refreeze the egg whites once again. You can store egg whites in the freezer for up to one year.
- Egg whites will not whip well in the presence of fat, so make sure the bowl and beaters are perfectly clean. If there is a particle of egg yolk or other matter in the whites, spoon it out.
- Egg whites, whether beaten to the soft peak or stiff peak stage, should never be dry. Well-beaten whites stand in glossy peaks. Do not overbeat the egg whites. Dry egg whites will clump when folded into sauces or other mixtures.

AMARETTO SOUFFLE

1 envelope (1 Tbsp.) unflavored gelatin
1 cup water
4 oz. Neufchatel cheese/low calorie cream cheese
¾ tsp. almond extract
16 packets (16 grams) EQUAL® Tabletop Sweetener, divided
2 egg whites
1 cup non-dairy whipped topping

Combine gelatin and water in a small saucepan. Cook over low heat until gelatin is dissolved. Blend Neufchatel cheese in a bowl until it is smooth. Add cheese to gelatin mixture. Cook the mixture over low heat, stirring constantly until it is smooth. Remove from heat. Stir in almond extract and 12 packets of Equal. Chill until mixture is the consistency of unbeaten egg whites. Beat egg whites until soft peaks form. Add 4 packets Equal and continue beating until stiff peaks form. Fold egg whites and nondairy whipped topping together. Fold egg white mixture into cream cheese mixture. Pour into souffle dish. Chill until firm.

Garnish with strawberry slices and/or chopped almonds.

Servings: 6
Exchanges: 1 Fat and ½ Milk
Calories: 103

APRICOT SOUFFLE

2 cans (16 oz. each) apricot halves, packed in unsweetened juice, drained
4 eggs
3 egg yolks
⅛ tsp. salt
12 packets (12 grams) EQUAL® Tabletop Sweetener
2 envelopes (2 Tbsp.) unflavored gelatin
¼ cup lemon juice
¼ cup cold water
½ tsp. vanilla extract
¼ tsp. almond extract
1 tsp. rum extract
½ cup evaporated skim milk

Puree apricots in food processor or blender and set aside. (Reserve one apricot half for garnish.) Using electric mixer, beat eggs, yolks, salt, and Equal at high speed for approximately 15 minutes or until mixture is very thick and creamy. While eggs are beating, place gelatin, lemon juice, and cold water in saucepan. Heat and stir until dissolved. Remove from heat and set aside. When eggs are thoroughly beaten, add extracts. Continue beating and add dissolved gelatin. Turn mixer to low and add apricot puree. Transfer mixture to another bowl. In chilled bowl, beat cold evaporated skim milk until stiff peaks form. Fold into apricot mixture. Pour into 6-cup souffle dish with a 3-inch aluminum foil collar. Refrigerate.

Garnish by cutting the apricot half into 10 very thin slices and fanning the slices on the soufle.

Servings: 10
Exchanges: 1 Meat and 1 Fruit
Calories: 90

CHOCOLATE MOUSSE

1 cup skim milk
1 envelope (1 Tbsp.) unflavored gelatin
2 squares (2 oz.) unsweetened baking chocolate
2 egg yolks
⅛ tsp. salt
1 tsp. vanilla extract
24 packets (24 grams) EQUAL® Table Sweetener
2 egg whites
½ cup instant nonfat dry milk or ½ cup evaporated skim milk

Combine milk and gelatin, and let stand until gelatin softtens. Melt chocolate in a medium saucepan over low heat. Stir milk mixture into chocolate, then add egg yolks and salt. Stir the mixture over medium heat until it thickens. Remove from heat and add vanilla and Equal. Cool. Beat egg whites until stiff peaks form, set aside. If using powdered milk, beat with ½ cup cold water until stiff peaks form. If using evaporated skim milk, beat until stiff peaks form but do not add water. Fold cooled chocolate mixture into egg whites, then fold in whipped milk. Pour into serving dish and refrigerate.

Garnish with a dollop of whipped topping, a sprinkling of chopped nuts, or a slice of kiwi fruit.

Servings: 8
Exchanges: 1 Meat and 1 Fruit
Calories: 106

CHOCOLATE PUDDING ♡

⅓ cup cocoa powder
3 Tbsp. cornstarch
¼ tsp. salt
2½ cups skim milk
12 packets (12 grams) EQUAL® Tabletop Sweetener
1 tsp. vanilla extract

Sift cocoa into medium saucepan to remove lumps, then mix in cornstarch and salt. Slowly stir in milk. Cook mixture over medium heat, stirring constantly until it begins to boil and thicken. Turn heat to low and continue cooking and stirring for 3 minutes. Remove from heat and add Equal and vanilla. Pour into custard cups and place a sheet of plastic wrap on surface of each pudding to prevent skin from forming. Chill.

Garnish with a few very thin slices of banana and a dollop of whipped topping. Or use Coconut Cream Sauce (page 40). It adds a fresh touch to an old favorite.

Servings: 6
Exchanges: 1 Bread
Calories: 69

CUSTARD

4 eggs
3 cups skim milk
12 packets (12 grams) EQUAL® Tabletop Sweetener
1 pinch salt
1 tsp. vanilla extract
1 pinch nutmeg

Beat eggs well, then stir in milk, Equal, salt, and vanilla. Pour mixture into eight custard cups and sprinkle each with nutmeg. Place cups in a large pan with a cover and pour water into the pan up to the level of the custard in the cups. (Be careful not to get water in the cups.) Place pan on stove over high heat and bring water to a boil. Once water boils, reduce heat to medium, cover pan, and cook until custards are set (30-45 minutes). Check frequently for doneness near end of cooking time by inserting a knife blade into one of the custards. If the knife blade is clean when you remove it, the custard is done.

Garnish with one of the fruit sauces (see Chapter 3). Hot Buttered Rum Sauce (page 35), or Granola Topping (page 36).

Servings: 8
Exchanges: 1 Milk
Calories: 72

INSTANT ORANGE MOUSSE ♡

2/3 cup hot water
2 envelopes (2 Tbsp.) unflavored gelatin
2 packets (2 grams) EQUAL® Tabletop Sweetener
1 can (6 oz.) unsweetened orange juice concentrate, partially thawed
2 Tbsp. evaporated skim milk
½ tsp. vanilla extract
2 cups ice cubes

Pour hot water and gelatin into blender. Blend 30 seconds at lowest setting. Add Equal and continue blending 5 seconds longer. Add orange juice concentrate, evaporated skim milk, and vanilla. Turn blender to high setting, add ice cubes gradually, and blend until ice is evenly distributed in mixture. Pour into parfait glasses and chill. Keep refrigerated until immediately before serving.

Garnish with a whipped topping and a wedge of sliced orange.

Servings: 6
Exchanges: 1 Fruit
Calories: 40

MOCHA CHIFFON

⅓ cup cocoa powder
3 Tbsp. cornstarch
¼ tsp. salt
2 envelopes (2 Tbsp.) unflavored gelatin
2 tsp. instant coffee
2 egg yolks
2½ cups skim milk
18 packets (18 grams) EQUAL® Tabletop Sweetener, divided
1 cup low-fat cottage cheese
2 egg whites
½ cup low-fat plain yogurt

Combine cocoa, cornstarch, salt, gelatin, coffee, and egg in a medium saucepan. Stir in milk. Place over medium heat and stir until mixture thickens. Remove from heat, add 12 packets Equal, and bring to room temperature. Blend cottage cheese in blender at low setting or food processor until cheese is smooth and free of lumps. Add to cooled gelatin mixture and beat well. Beat egg whites until soft peaks form. Add Equal and beat until stiff peaks form. Fold into gelatin mixture. Fold in yogurt. Pour mixture into serving bowl or individual dishes and chill until firm.

Read labels to make sure you are indeed buying low-fat cottage cheese and plain yogurt.

Servings: 10
Exchanges: 1 Meat and 1 Fruit
Calories: 105

PINEAPPLE CHEESE DREAM

3 Tbsp. cornstarch
⅔ cup water
1 can (8 oz.) unsweetened crushed pineapple, undrained
1 tsp. grated lemon peel
2 Tbsp. lemon juice
2 egg yolks
3 oz. Neufchatel cheese/low calorie cream cheese.
10 packets (10 grams) EQUAL® Tabletop Sweetener
2 egg whites

Combine cornstarch and water in a medium saucepan. Stir until smooth and add pineapple. Cook over medium heat until mixture boils and thickens, stirring well. Remove from heat, stir in lemon juice, and beaten egg yolks. Add cheese. Return to heat and continue cooking and stirring until mixture bubbles. Remove from heat, add Equal, and beat with mixer to blend in cheese. Set aside to cool. Beat egg whites until soft peaks form. Fold into cooled pineapple mixture. Spoon into dessert dishes and refrigerate until served.

Serve this dessert in stemmed goblet for an elegant presentation.

Servings: 6
Exchanges: 1 Fruit and 1 Fat
Calories: 98

PUMPKIN PUDDING ♡

9 packets (9 grams) EQUAL® Tabletop Sweetener
3 Tbsp. cornstarch
½ tsp. ginger
1 tsp. cinnamon
¼ tsp. nutmeg
¼ tsp. ground cloves
¼ tsp. salt
1 cup canned pumpkin
1 can (13 oz.) evaporated skim milk

Mix all dry ingredients except Equal in a medium saucepan. Add pumpkin and milk and mix well. Cook and stir over medium heat until mixture comes to a boil. Turn heat to low and cook two minutes longer. Remove from heat and stir in Equal. Pour into serving dishes and cover with plastic wrap to prevent a skin from forming.

Garnish each serving with a spoonful of whipped topping and a dash of nutmeg. For added crunch, try a sprinking of Granola Topping (page 36).

Servings: 6
Exchanges: 1 Milk
Calories: 83

PUDDINGS, MOUSSES, AND SOUFFLES

RAISIN RICE PUDDING ♡

2 cups water
½ tsp. salt
½ cup. white rice, uncooked
¼ cup raisins
2 Tbsp. cornstarch
1¼ cups skim milk
1½ tsp. vanilla extract
6 packets (6 grams) EQUAL® Tabletop Sweetener

Bring water and salt to a boil in a medium saucepan. Stir in rice and raisins. Return to a boil, then reduce heat to low. Cover and cook 30 minutes. Mix cornstarch with milk, stirring well. Add slowly to rice mixture, mixing well. Continue cooking and stirring over low heat until mixture thickens. Remove from heat, add vanilla and Equal, and refrigerate.

Garnish with ground nutmeg, just like Grandma did!

Servings: 6
Exchanges: 1 Bread
Calories: 90

RASPBERRY YOGURT SUBLIME

1½ cups unsweetened raspberries, fresh or frozen
2 egg yolks
½ cup skim milk
1 envelope (1 Tbsp.) unflavored gelatin
15 packets (15 grams) EQUAL® Tabletop Sweetener, divided
1 cup plain low-fat yogurt
1 tsp. lemon juice
4 drops red food coloring (optional)
2 egg whites
1 8-inch or 9-inch Pastry Crust (page 81) or Graham Cracker Crust (page 80)

Puree raspberries in blender but reserve a few for garnish. Beat egg yolks with milk and mix with gelatin. Place mixture in medium saucepan and let stand for 1 minute. Stir over low heat until gelatin is completely dissolved, about 5 minutes. Remove from heat. With wire whip or rotary beater, blend in 9 packets Equal, pureed raspberries, yogurt, lemon juice, and food coloring. Chill, stirring occasionally, until mixture mounds slightly when dropped from a spoon. Beat egg whites in a medium bowl until soft peaks form. Gradually add 6 remaining packets and beat until stiff peaks form. Fold whites into gelatin mixture. Pour into Equal prepared crust and chill until firm.

Garnish with reserved raspberries. You may substitute boysenberries for the raspberries; if you do, omit the food coloring.

Servings: 8
Exchanges: ½ Milk (filling only)
½ Milk, 1 Bread, and 1 Fat (filling and Graham Cracker Crust)
½ Milk, 1 Bread, and 2 Fat (filling and Pastry Crust)
Calories: 59 (filling only)
179 (filling and Graham Cracker Crust)
219 (filling and Pastry Crust)

TAPIOCA PUDDING

3 Tbsp. tapioca
⅛ tsp. salt
2 cups skim milk
1 egg yolk
1 egg white
½ tsp. vanilla extract
5 packets (5 grams) EQUAL® Tabletop Sweetener

Mix tapioca, salt and egg yolk in pan. Let stand 5 minutes. Beat egg white until soft peaks form. Set aside. Cook tapioca mixture over medium heat to a full boil, stirring constantly. Gradually add the beaten egg white, stirring quickly until just blended. Remove from heat, add vanilla and Equal. Cool 20 minutes. Stir. Serve warm or chilled.

Garnish with any colorful fresh or frozen unsweetened fruit (sliced peaches, berries, oranges, and so on). If you wish to omit the egg yolk, add 1 drop yellow food coloring.

Sevings: 5
Exchanges: 1 Milk
Calories: 69

VANILLA PUDDING

5 Tbsp. cornstarch
¼ tsp. salt
3 cups skim milk
3 egg yolks
1 Tbsp. vanilla
12 packets (12 grams) EQUAL® Tabletop Sweetener

Mix cornstarch and salt in a medium saucepan. Gradually add milk and stir well. Cook and stir over medium heat until mixture boils. Continue cooking one minute, then remove from heat and stir about half of hot mixture into beaten egg yolks. Mix well and return egg mixture to saucepan. Cook and stir one more minute. Remove from heat. Stir in vanilla and Equal. Pour into serving dishes, cover with plastic wrap, and bring to room temperature. Refrigerate.

Garnish with Strawberry Topping (page 33) or Cherry Rum Sauce (page 41). Serve on Valentie's Day or the Fourth of July.

Servings: 6
Exchanges: 1 Milk
Calories: 103

LEMON PUDDING ♡

½ cup lemon juice
3 Tbsp. cornstarch
⅛ tsp. salt
2 cups skim milk
few drops yellow food coloring
few drops lemon extract
12 packets (12 grams) EQUAL® Tabletop Sweetener

Mix lemon juice, cornstarch, and salt in a medium saucepan and stir until smooth. Add milk. Place over medium heat and stir until mixture boils and thickens. Remove from heat and stir in food color, lemon extract, and Equal. Pour into dessert dishes and cover with plastic wrap to prevent a skin from forming. Refrigerate.

Garnish with Brandied Blackberry Sauce (page 32) or Cherry Rum Sauce (page 41) for an interesting flavor contrast.

Servings: 4
Exchanges: 1 Bread
Calories: 75

HINTS TO MAKE YOUR SAUCES, TOPPINGS, AND FILLINGS A SUCCESS

Sauces, toppings, and fillings are usually loaded with sugar and empty calories. These versions provide great taste and visual appeal at a fraction of the calories. Read the serving suggestions to get an idea of the versatility of these recipes. But don't let the suggestions limit you—be creative!

Cornstarch is the ingredient that thickens many of these sauces. Lower in calories than flour, cornstarch will make your finished sauce glisten. To use cornstarch correctly, be sure to dissolve it well in a small amount of cold water before adding it to the sauce. Cornstarch added directly to the sauce will produce a lumpy texture. Your sauce will need to come to a full boil for the cornstarch to thicken properly.

You may substitute equal amounts of arrowroot for cornstarch.

Sauces need constant stirring, or they will stick and scorch on the bottom of the pan. If you like, use a double boiler as an added precaution.

These sauce recipes have lots of delicious uses. They are great on waffles or pancakes, French toast, yogurt, fruits, custards, pound cake, and angel food cake. Or spread them between graham crackers. Use your imagination!

If you prepare a sauce ahead, be sure it is thoroughly cooled before you store it in an airtight container. If you cover a sauce while it's still hot, condensed moisture in the container will thin your sauce.

Many of these recipes are easily adapted for use in the microwave oven.

SAUCES, TOPPINGS, AND FILLINGS

BRANDIED BLACKBERRY SAUCE ♡

1 package (16 oz.) frozen unsweetened blackberries, with juice
2 Tbsp. cornstarch
6 packets (6 grams) EQUAL® Tabletop Sweetener
2 Tbsp. brandy

Defrost berries and drain, reserving juice. Add water to juice to equal one cup. Dissolve cornstarch in a small amount of juice, then add remaining juice. Heat juice in a medium saucepan over medium heat, until mixture comes to a boil and thickens. Remove from heat. Stir in berries, Equal, and brandy. Cool thoroughly before refrigerating.

Substitute strawberries for blackberries. Try this sauce on Lemon Pudding (page 29), Dessert Crepes (page 103), angel food cake, or a small scoop of vanilla ice cream.

Yield: 2 cups
Servings: 8 (¼-cup) servings
Exchanges: 1 Fruit
Calories: 36

VANILLA CREAM SAUCE OR FILLING

1 egg
3 Tbsp. flour
¼ tsp. salt
1¼ cups skim milk
12 packets (12 grams) EQUAL® Tabletop Sweetener
1 tsp. vanilla extract

Lightly beat egg and set aside. Combine flour and salt in a small saucepan. Gradually add milk, mixing well. Cook and stir over medium heat until mixture boils. Boil 1 minute. Blend small amount of hot mixture into beaten egg, then add egg mixture to saucepan. Mix well. Continue cooking until mixture thickens, stirring con-

SAUCES, TOPPINGS, AND FILLINGS

stantly. Remove from heat, stir in Equal and vanilla. Cool, then refrigerate.

Spread between graham crackers for your own sandwich cookies.

Yield: 1½ cups
Servings: 6 (¼-cup) servings
12 (2-Tbsp.) servings
Exchanges: 1 Fruit per ¼ cup
½ Fruit per 2 Tbsp.
Calories: 26 per 2 Tbsp.
52 per ¼ cup

STRAWBERRY TOPPING ♡

3 cups unsweetened strawberries, fresh or frozen
½ envelope (1½ tsp.) unflavored gelatin
1½ tsp. lemon juice
4 packages (4 grams) EQUAL® Tabletop Sweetener

Put the strawberries in a saucepan. Cook, covered, over very low heat without water for about 10 minutes. Remove the lid and bring the fruit to the boiling point. Boil for 1 minute and remove from heat. Soften the gelatin in lemon juice. Pour some of the hot juice from the strawberries into the gelatin. Stir until the gelatin is completely dissolved. Add Equal and the dissolved gelatin to the strawberries. Cool to room temperature, then refrigerate.

You can use this recipe for any fresh fruit topping, especially peaches, pineapple, and berries of all types. Leftovers are great on pancakes or French toast. You will need this topping to make Trifle (page 108).

Yield: 1¼ cups
Servings: 12 (2-Tbsp.) servings
Exchanges: FREE per 2 Tbsp.
Calories: 18 per 2 Tbsp.

PINEAPPLE SAUCE OR FILLING

1 can (8 oz.) unsweetened crushed pineapple
¼ tsp. salt
3 Tbsp. cornstarch
2 egg yolks, slightly beaten
6 packets (6 grams) EQUAL® Tabletop Sweetener

Drain pineapple, reserving liquid. If necessary, add water to reserved liquid to equal ¾ cup. Combine salt and cornstarch in a small saucepan. Gradually stir in liquid and mix well. Place mixture over medium heat and stir until it boils. Boil 1 minute. Blend small amount of hot mixture into egg yolks, then return to saucepan. Mix well. Stir in pineapple and continue cooking until mixture begins to thicken, stirring constantly. Remove from heat, add Equal, cool, and refrigerate.

Try this sauce on custard, crepes, or a small scoop of vanilla ice cream. Dress up waffles and French toast with Pineapple Sauce.

Yield: 1½ cups
Servings: 12 (2-Tbsp.) servings
Exchanges: FREE per 2 Tbsp.
Calories: 17 per 2 Tbsp.

LEMON SAUCE ♡

3 Tbsp. cornstarch
½ cup water
½ cup lemon juice
⅛ tsp. salt
3-4 drops yellow food coloring (optional)
12 packets (12 *grams*) EQUAL® Tabletop Sweetener

Combine starch with water and lemon juice in a small saucepan, and stir until smooth. Add salt and optional food coloring. Cook over low heat until mixture thickens, stirring frequently. Remove from heat and add Equal. Serve warm or cold.

Serve over fresh fruit or angel food cake.

Yield: 1 cup
Servings (8 (2-Tbsp.) servings
Exchanges: FREE per 2 Tbsp.
Calories: 15 per 2 Tbsp.

BUTTERED RUM SAUCE

1 Tbsp. plus 2 tsp. cornstarch
⅛ tsp. salt
1 cup water
2 Tbsp. margarine
2 Tbsp. light cream (half and half)
1 tsp. vanilla extract
1 tsp. rum extract
12 packets (12 grams) EQUAL® Tabletop Sweetener

Mix cornstrach and salt in a small saucepan. Stir in water. Place over medium heat and stir until mixture thickens and clears, about 5 minutes. Remove from heat and stir in margarine, cream, vanilla, rum extract, and Equal. Stir until margarine melts. Serve warm; or cool, then refrigerate until needed.

Serve on custard, fruit, or hot baked apples.

Yield: 1½ cups
Exchanges: ½ Fat
Calories: 32

GRANOLA TOPPING ♡

*microwave too!

6 Tbsp. margarine
1 tsp. ground cinnamon
¼ cup all-purpose flour
1 cup granola, plain unsweetened
16 packets (16 grams) EQUAL® Tabletop Sweetener

Conventional Method   Melt margarine in a small saucepan over medium-low heat. Stir in cinnamon, flour, and granola (crush any lumps). Place mixture on a cookie sheet and bake at 350 degrees, uncovered, until granola is crisp and flavors are well blended. Remove from oven and stir in Equal. Allow to stand about 5 minutes and then break up into smaller pieces. Cool completely; store in an airtight container.

Microwave Method   Place margarine in a large glass pie plate or shallow glass baking dish. Microwave on high setting 3 minutes or until bubbly. Stir in cinnamon, flour, and granola (crush any lumps). Cook uncovered 2-4 minutes or until granola is crisp and flavors are well blended. Remove from oven and stir in Equal. Allow to stand about 5 minutes and then break up into smaller pieces. Cool completely; store in an airtight container.

Serve this healthful crunchy topping on fruit, fruit pies, yogurt, or ice cream. Try this on Pumpkin Pudding (page 24) too!

Yield: 1½ cups
Servings: 12 (2-Tbsp.) servings
Exchanges: FREE per 2 tsp.
½ Bread and 1 Fat per 3 Tbsp.
Calories: 16 per 2 tsp.
75 per 3 Tbsp.

FUDGE SAUCE ♡

2 cups skim milk
1 Tbsp. cocoa powder
¼ tsp. chocolate extract
2 tsp. cornstarch
1 square (1 oz.) unsweetened baking chocolate
7 packets (7 grams) EQUAL® Tabletop Sweetener

Mix all ingredients except chocolate and Equal, stirring to remove all lumps. When no lumps remain, place over low heat and stir in chocolate. Cook until mixture thickens. Remove from heat and add Equal.

Serve over mint sherbet or eclairs or as a special dip for fresh strawberries. Try the Fudge Sauce between graham crackers for a "creme sandwich." Use your imagination!

Yield: 2 cups
Servings: 16 (2-Tbsp.) servings
Exchanges: FREE
Calories: 20

SAUCES, TOPPINGS, AND FILLINGS

CUSTARD SAUCE ♡

3 eggs
9 packets (9 grams) EQUAL® Tabletop Sweetener
1 pinch salt
2½ cups skim milk
1 tsp. vanilla extract

Beat eggs briefly. Blend beaten eggs, and salt in top of double boiler. (Place hot water in bottom of double boiler, but do not let top pan touch water.) Add milk in a thin stream, stirring constantly, and cook over medium heat until mixture coats a metal spoon. (Water in double boiler should not boil.) Remove top of double boiler from heat; stir vanilla and Equal into custard. Place top of double boiler in cold water until custard cools. (If custard curdles, beat vigorously with rotary beater until smooth.) Cover, chill 2-3 hours.

Serve over Eclairs (page 104), fruit, angel food cake, or a hot fruit crisp.

Yield: 3 cups
Servings: 12 (¼-cup) servings
Exchanges: ½ Meat and ½ Milk
Calories: 40

CRANBERRY SAUCE ♡

1 cup water
1 cup unsweetened cranberries, fresh or frozen
24 packets (24 grams) EQUAL® Tabletop Sweetener

Boil water in a stainless steel or an enameled small saucepan, then add cranberries. Boil without stirring until all the skins pop open, about 5 minutes. Remove from heat, add Equal, and cool to room temperature. Chill if desired.

This sauce makes a light dessert as well as a garnish for meats.

Yield: 1¼ cups

Servings: 5 (¼-cup) servings
Exchanges: FREE
Calories: 23

CRANBERRY ORANGE RELISH ♡

4 cups (1 lb.) unsweetened cranberries, fresh or frozen
1 medium navel orange
18-24 packets (18-24 grams) EQUAL® Tabletop Sweetener

Chop cranberries finely. Peel orange and chop the flesh into small pieces. Mix together and add Equal. You may add more to make the relish sweeter. Cover and chill.

This is a dessert for the day you thought you didn't have any calories left to spend! Many people like the taste of orange rind in this relish. If you wish, chop the orange rind and add it as well.

Yield: 3½ cups
Exchanges: FREE per ½ cup
Calories: 15

COCONUT CREAM SAUCE OR FILLING ♡

1 egg
3 Tbsp. flour
¼ tsp. salt
1¼ cups skim milk
12 packets (12 grams) EQUAL® Tabletop Sweetener
1 tsp. vanilla extract
⅓ cup shredded coconut

Lightly beat egg, set aside. Combine flour and salt in a small saucepan. Gradually add milk, mix well. Place over medium heat and stir until mixture boils. Boil 1 minute. Blend small amount of hot mixture into beaten egg, then add egg mixture to saucepan. Mix well. Continue cooking until mixture thickens, stirring constantly. Remove from heat, stir in Equal, vanilla, and coconut. Cool, then refrigerate.

This sauce is great on a tropical fruit mixture, such as pineapple, kiwi, or banana.

Yield: 1½ cups
Servings: 8 (3-Tbsp.) servings
Exchanges: 1 Fruit
Calories: 51

CHOCOLATE CREAM SAUCE OR FILLING ♡

1 egg
3 Tbsp. flour
¼ tsp. salt
1¼ cups skim milk
18 packets (18 grams) EQUAL® Tabletop Sweetener
1 tsp. vanilla extract
1 square (1 oz.) unsweetened baking chocolate

Lightly beat egg, set aside. Combine flour and salt in a small saucepan. Gradually add milk and mix well. Place over medium heat and stir until mixture boils. Boil 1 minute. Blend small amount of hot mixture into beaten egg, then add egg mixture to saucepan. Mix well. Continue cooking until mixture bubbles, stirring constantly. Remove from heat; add vanilla, and chocolate; and stir until chocolate melts. Bring to room temperature before refrigerating.

Serve as a great fondue for squares of angel food cake and fresh fruit chunks.

Yield: 1½ cups
Servings: 12 (2-Tbsp.) servings
Exchanges: ½ Fruit and ½ Fat
Calories: 40

CHERRY RUM SAUCE ♡

1½ tsp. cornstarch
½ cup water
1 cup frozen cherries, unsweetened
5 packets (5 grams) EQUAL® Tabletop Sweetener
½ tsp. rum extract

Dissolve cornstarch in water in a small saucepan. Add cherries. Heat and stir constantly until mixture thickens. Remove from heat and add Equal and rum extract. Bring to room temperature before refrigerating.

Excellent on Custard (page 20), Dessert Crepes (page 103), Vanilla Air (page 61), Lemon Pudding (page 29) and Vanilla Pudding (page 28).

Yield: 1½ cups
Servings: 12 (2 Tbsp.) servings
Exchanges: FREE per 2 Tbsp.
Calories: 12 per 2 Tbsp.

HINTS TO MAKE YOUR FRUIT SALAD DESSERTS A SUCCESS

We've made the traditional dieter's dessert even better. Because you can use frozen fruit in many of these recipes, you can enjoy colorful, appealing fruit desserts the year round.

Double check the packaged fruits you purchase to be sure they are unsweetened.

Frozen packaged fruits purchased in bulk are great to use because you simply pour out what you need, then reseal the bag and save the rest for later.

When cutting sticky foods, such as dried fruits, dip the knife in hot water for easier cutting.

Don't forget to dip cut bananas and apples in lemon juice to prevent discoloration.

Cranberries are easy to grind when frozen. Wash the berries, pat them dry, and freeze until ready to use.

If you purchase fruits that are not quite fully ripe, store them at room temperature in a fruit-ripening bowl or a loosely closed brown paper bag.

APRICOT FRUIT COMPOTE ♡

*microwave too!

½ lb. dried apricots
1 cup white raisins
1½ cups water
2 Tbsp. lemon juice
8 packets (8 grams) EQUAL® Tabletop Sweetener
1 can (11 oz.) unsweetened mandarin oranges, drained

Conventional Method Rinse apricots and raisins and drain. Put apricots and raisins in a 2-quart saucepan. Add water and cook, uncovered, until fruit is tender. Add lemon juice, Equal, and mandarin oranges. Heat thoroughly. Let stand 2 or 3 minutes before serving.

Microwave Method Rinse apricots and raisins and drain. Put apricots and raisins in a 1½-quart casserole. Add water and cook, uncovered, on high setting for 5 minutes. Add lemon juice, Equal, and mandarin oranges. Cook on high setting 5 minutes longer. Let stand 2 or 3 minutes before serving.

Add a delicious crunch with Granola Topping, page 36. For a homespun look, serve in stoneware or pottery.

Servings: 12
Exchanges: 2 Fruit
Calories: 93

CINNAMON GLAZED PINEAPPLE ♡

*microwave too!

1 can (13½ oz.) unsweetened pineapple tidbits
3 packets (3 grams) EQUAL® Tabletop Sweetener
1 Tbsp. cornstarch
¼ tsp. cinnamon
2 Tbsp. margarine

Conventional Method Put pineapple in a 1-quart saucepan. Mix Equal, cornstarch, and cinnamon and add to pineapple, stirring well. Cut margarine in 2 pieces and add to pineapple. Cook over medium heat until pineapple is tender, approximately 15 minutes, stirring constantly. Serve hot.

Microwave Method Put pineapple in a 1-quart casserole. Mix Equal, cornstarch, and cinnamon in a small cup. Add to pineapple, stirring well. Cut margarine in 2 pieces and place over top. Cover. Microwave at high setting for 6-7 minutes, stirring well after 3 minutes. Serve hot.

Serve warm and sprinkle with cinnamon.

Yield: 1⅔ cups
Servings: 4
Exchanges: 2 Fruit
Calories: 97

FRUIT PIE ♡

*microwave too!

1½ cups warm water
2 envelopes (2 Tbsp.) unflavored gelatin
½ tsp. lemon extract
½ tsp. grated lemon peel
1 packet (1 gram) EQUAL® Tabletop Sweetener
¼ tsp. margarine to grease pan
1 graham cracker square (2-inch), crushed
2 fresh peaches, peeled and sliced
2 cups sliced fresh strawberries
2 cups fresh blueberries

Conventional Method Combine water and gelatin in a 1-quart saucepan. Heat until gelatin dissolves. Stir lemon extract, lemon peel, and Equal into gelatin mixture. Set aside. Grease an 8- or 9 inch pie plate with margarine. Sprinkle graham crumbs over bottom of plate. Layer sliced peaches in pie plate. Top with one third of gelatin mixture, then strawberries and blueberries. Cover with remaining gelatin mixture. Refrigerate about 2-4 hours or until completely set.

Microwave Method Combine water and gelatin in a 1-quart measure. Microwave on high setting for 1½ minutes or until mixture is heated and gelatin dissolves. Stir lemon extract, lemon peel, and Equal into gelatin mixture. Set aside. Grease an 8- or 9-inch pie plate with margarine. Top with one third of gelatin mixture, then strawberries and blueberries. Cover with remaining gelatin mixture. Refrigerate about 2-4 hours or until completely set.

Garnish with lemon slices.

Servings: 8
Exchanges: 1 Fruit
Calories: 55

FRUIT DESSERTS

APPLE CRISP ♡

*microwave only

8 apples, pared and sliced
8 packets (8 grams) EQUAL® Tabletop Sweetener
2 Tbsp. flour
½ tsp. cinnamon
1 Tbsp. margarine
2 Tbsp. Lemon Juice

Topping:
6 packets (6 grams) EQUAL® Tabletop Sweetener
½ cup flour
⅓ cup margarine
a pinch of salt

Arrange apple slices in an 8 × 8 inch glass baking dish.

Mix together the EQUAL® Tabletop Sweetener, flour and cinnamon. Cut in the margarine. Sprinkle this flour mixture over the apples. Sprinkle lemon juice over all.

To prepare topping: Mix all the ingredients together until crumbly. Sprinkle over the apples, then pat until firm on top.

Microwave on high, uncovered, 15 minutes, turning dish every 5 minutes. Let stand 15 minutes and serve.

A dollop of whipped topping would make a special finish to a warm serving of apple crisp. Even more delightful with a hot spiced tea!

Servings: 16
Exchanges: 1 Fruit, 1 Fat and ½ Bread
Calories: 123

PEARS IN CUSTARD

*microwave only

4 small fresh pears
½ cup water
12 packets (12 grams) EQUAL® Tabletop Sweetener, divided
1½ cups skim milk
3 eggs
⅛ tsp. salt
1 tsp. vanilla extract

Peel and halve the pears. Place in a glass dish. Mix the water and 8 packets Equal together; add to pears in glass dish. Microwave on high setting, uncovered, 8 minutes, turning dish and stirring gently 3 times. Let stand 3 minutes outside of oven. Remove pears from liquid with a perforated spoon. Place a half pear in each of 8 dessert dishes. Pour milk into a 1-quart casserole or 4-cup measure, microwave on high setting for 4 minutes. Beat eggs until frothy, slowly add 4 remainaing packets Equal and salt, and beat until fluffy. Gradually add scalded milk and vanilla, stirring constantly. Pour an equal amount of custard liquid over each pear. Pour 1 cup boiling water into an 8-×-8-inch baking dish and carefully set 4 dessert dishes in it. Bake 4-5 minutes, uncovered, turning dishes every minute until custard is barely set. (It thickens quite a bit when cold.) Repeat process with remaining desserts. Refrigerate until ready to serve.

Try Cherry Rum Sauce (page 41) or a Brandied Blackberry Sauce (page 32) as a topping for this delicate custard.

Servings: 8
Exchanges: ½ Fruit and ½ Milk or 1 Bread
Calories: 69

FRUIT DESSERTS

SAUCY RHUBARB ♡

*microwave too!

2 cups water
1 lb. fresh or unsweetened frozen rhubarb, diced into ½-inch pieces
24 packets (24 grams) EQUAL® Tabletop Sweetener

Conventional Method Boil 2 cups water. Add rhubarb and simmer gently without stirring until rhubarb is tender when pierced with fork (about 8 minutes). Stir in the Equal. (Stir gently, rhubarb should remain in distinct pieces.) Chill and serve.

Microwave Method Place rhubarb and water in a 2-quart casserole. Cook for 4-5 minutes, covered, stirring once. Remove from oven and add Equal. Let stand 3 minutes. Stir gently but thoroughly. Chill and serve.

Remember, rhubarb tastes much sweeter when cold. You can add more Equal to the cooked rhubarb if necessary. Rhubarb is one dessert you can have when you can't afford any extra calories.

Yield: 4 cups
Servings: 8 (½-cup) servings
Exchanges: FREE per 1 cup
Calories: 8 per ½ cup

STRAWBERRY RHUBARB COMPOTE ♡

*microwave too!

4 cups (20-oz. package) frozen rhubarb, cut into 1-inch pieces
½ tsp. cinnamon
¼ cup water
2 cups sliced fresh strawberries
6 packets (6 grams) EQUAL® Tabletop Sweetener
5 drops red food coloring

Conventional Method Combine rhubarb, cinnamon, and water in a large sauce pan. Cover. Cook over medium heat until rhubarb is tender, stirring occasionally. Mash rhubarb slightly. Stir in strawberries, Equal, and food coloring. Heat thoroughly. Serve chilled.

Microwave Method Combine rhubarb, cinnamon and water in a large casserole. Cover. Microwave on high setting for 12 minutes or until rhubarb is tender, stirring 2-3 times. Mash rhubarb slightly. Stir in strawberries, Equal and food coloring. Microwave on medium (50 percent) setting 1 minute or until strawberries are heated. Serve chilled.

Try this compote on a slice of angel food cake for a colorful low-calorie treat.

Servings: 6 (½-cup) servings
Exchanges: 1 Fruit
Calories: 36

TUTTI FRUITTY DESSERT ♡

1 can (11 oz.) unsweetened mandarin oranges
1½ cups orange juice
2 envelopes (2 Tbsp.) unflavored gelatin
6 packets (6 grams) EQUAL® Tabletop Sweetener
2 cups (16 oz.) plain low-fat yogurt
1 apple, diced into bite-size pieces
1 cup blueberries, unsweetened

Drain mandarin oranges and remove juice. Heat orange juice to boiling point. Mix unflavored gelatin and Equal in a large bowl; add hot juice and stir until gelatin is completely dissolved. With wire whisk or rotary beater, blend in yogurt and reserved juice from canned oranges. Chill, stirring occasionally, until mixture is consistency of unbeaten egg whites. Stir in oranges, apple, and blueberries. Pour into 11-x-7-inch pan and chill until firm. To serve, cut into 12 squares.

Garnish with Granola Topping (page 36). You can substitute any fruits (except pineapple, papaya, mango and kiwi) for the mandarin oranges, apple, and blueberries. You need 3 cups of total of fruit.

Servings: 12
Exchanges: 1 Fruit
Calories: 46

HINTS TO MAKE YOUR FROZEN DESSERTS A SUCCESS

Icy, frosty, refreshing — these are the words you'll use to describe the delightful frozen desserts in this chapter. The child in you, and the children who live with you, will love these cool treats.

To speed up the freezing process, start with well-chilled ingredients.

Store frozen desserts in the coldest part of your freezer — usually that's the back bottom shelf, away from the door.

For initial freezing, use a shallow cake pan, or ice cube trays. Mixing bowls or deep containers delay freezing. When your dessert is ready for final freezing, use any mold or dish.

One way to assure fine texture in your frozen desserts is to stir the mixture occasionally during the initial freezing process. The more you stir, the finer the texture will be.

Freeze the dessert in individual dishes for ease of serving.

If you prepare your dessert well ahead of serving time, store it in a tightly covered container.

Before serving a frozen dessert, let it stand at room temperature for 5-10 minutes.

To keep your desserts frosty, prechill your serving cups or plates.

APPLE SORBET ♡

¾ cup unsweetened apple juice
12 packets (12 grams) EQUAL® Tabletop Sweetener
3 large, tart apples (such as Granny Smith), peeled, cored, and sliced
¼ cup lemon juice
2 Tbsp. apple jack brandy
pinch each of cinnamon, nutmeg, and salt

Place unsweetened apple juice in small bowl, add Equal, and chill. Meanwhile, puree apples in a blender or food processor. Mix with lemon juice, brandy, cinnamon, nutmeg, and salt. Fold in chilled apple juice. For a smooth, fine texture, freeze in hand-cranked or automatic ice cream freezer. You may pour into a refrigerator tray and freeze 2 hours or until firm, stirring occasionally. Cover with waxed paper to prevent crystals from forming. Spoon into chilled bowl; beat until fluffy. Return to tray and freeze until firm (2-3 hours).

Serve in parfait glass and garnish with a slice of strawberry if you wish.

Servings: 8
Exchanges: 1 Fruit
Calories: 52

BLUEBERRY ICE ♡

½ envelope (1½ tsp.) unflavored gelatin
1½ cups water, divided
1 package (10 oz.) unsweetened frozen blueberries, thawed (1½ cups)
3 Tbsps. lemon juice
6 packets (6 grams) EQUAL® Tabletop Sweetener

Combine gelatin and 1 cup water in a medium saucepan. Place over medium heat and stir until gelatin dissolves. Remove from heat, add remaining water, berries, lemon juice and Equal. Freeze until firm. Break into chunks, beat with mixer until smooth. Return to tray, freeze until firm. Let stand at room temperature 5-10 minutes before serving.

Try making this ice with raspberries, blackberries, strawberries, or a combination of berries.

Servings: 4
Exchanges: 1 Fruit
Calories: 40

CHERRY YOGURT FREEZE ♡

20 cherries, frozen or fresh pitted
2 cups plain low-fat yogurt
4 packets (4 grams) EQUAL® Tabletop Sweetener

Chop cherries (unthawed, if frozen) in a blender or food processor. Add yogurt and Equal and blend on low setting until smooth. Freeze until firm.

Garnish with a fresh or frozen cherry and a sprig of fresh mint.

Servings: 4 (½-cup) servings
Exchanges: ½ Milk and ½ Fruit
Calories: 84

DOUBLE-LAYER CHOCOLATE FREEZE

3 squares (3 oz.) unsweetened baking chocolate
1/3 cup water
12 packets (12 grams) EQUAL® Tabletop Sweetener
1/8 tsp. salt
1 can (13 oz.) evaporated skim milk, chilled
1 tsp. vanilla extract
2 egg yolks

Stirring constantly, melt chocolate and water in top of double boiler over hot water. Stir in Equal and salt. Set chocolate aside to cool. In a large bowl with mixer at high speed, beat milk and vanilla until stiff peaks form. Stir egg yolks into chocolate mixture. Fold chocolate into whipped milk until well combined. Pour into 8-ounce parfait glasses or dessert dishes and freeze until firm, at least 4 hours. When frozen, this dessert separates into two layers.

Garnish with whipped topping and serve in clear glass dish or glass so the double layers will show.

Number of Servings: 8
Calories: 109
Exchanges: 1/2 Milk and 1 Fat

CITRUS FROZEN DESSERT ♡

2 egg whites at room temperature
¼ cup frozen orange juice concentrate
2 packets (2 grams) EQUAL® Tabletop Sweetener
1⅓ cups graham cracker crumbs or 16 (2-inch) squares, crushed
6 Tbsp. soft margarine
4 Tbsp. finely chopped walnuts
1 cup plain low-fat yogurt

Beat egg whites with frozen orange juice and Equal seven minutes with electric beater at medium speed. Meanwhile, combine cracker crumbs and margarine and stir in chopped nuts. Press crumb mixture on bottom and sides of a 9-inch square baking pan. When the egg-orange mixture is beaten, fold in yogurt. Pour into baking dish and place in freezer at least 15 minutes.

Garnish with drained, unsweetened mandarin oranges and a sprinkling of chopped nuts.

Servings: 8
Exchanges: 3 Fat and 1 Bread
Calories: 209

CRANBERRY SORBET ♡

4 cups (1 lb) unsweetened cranberries, fresh or frozen
1¼ cups water, divided
¼ cup orange juice
2 Tbsp. lemon juice
18 packets (18 grams) EQUAL® Tabletop Sweetener

Puree cranberries and ¼ cup water in a blender or food processor until mixture is smooth and well blended. You may add slightly more than ¼ cup water if necessary to attain smooth texture. Bring remaining cup of water to a boil in a stainless steel or enameled saucepan. Stir in cranberry puree, orange juice, and lemon juice and lower heat at once. Simmer until puree is very smooth and has turned bright and shiny, about 5 minutes. Stir in the Equal. Cool to room temperature, stirring occasionally. Pour mixture into shallow pan and freeze until sorbet is frozen 1 inch in from edge. Turn cranberry mixture into a large, chilled bowl and beat sorbet at medium speed with chilled beaters. Put sorbet in tightly covered container or mold and freeze solid.

You can also use a manual or electric ice cream freezer to make this sorbet. Follow the manufacturer's directions.

Servings: 6
Exchanges: 1 Fruit
Calories: 38

FROZEN ESPRESSO ♡

4 cups espresso coffee
EQUAL® Tabletop Sweetener to taste

Place coffee in bowl and sweeten to taste with Equal. Freeze, stirring frequently, until set, about 2-3 hours. It is best to stir at 15-minute intervals. The more you stir, the finer the texture will be.

Serve with a dollop of whipped evaporated skim milk.

Servings: 4
Exchanges: FREE
Calories: 12

FROZEN LEMON DESSERT

18 vanilla wafers or 12 (2-inch) graham cracker squares, crushed and divided
1 Tbsp. grated lemon peel
⅛ tsp. salt
¼ cup lemon juice
3 egg yolks
3 egg whites
12 packets (12 grams) EQUAL® Tabletop Sweetener, divided
½ cup evaporated skim milk, chilled

Line 8-inch square pan with half of the cracker crumbs. Blend lemon peel, salt, lemon juice, and egg yolks in a small saucepan. Cook over medium heat until mixture thickens, stirring constantly. Remove from heat, add 6 packets Equal, and cool. Beat egg whites until frothy, gradually add 6 packets Equal, and continue to beat until whites form stiff peaks. Then beat the chilled evaporated skim milk until stiff peaks form. Fold beaten egg whites and whipped milk into chilled lemon mixture. Pour into prepared pan, top with remaining crumbs. Freeze about 4 hours or until set.

You will be thrilled with the generous portions this recipe yields.

Servings: 6 large!
Exchanges: 1 Bread and 1 Meat or 1 Milk and 1 Fruit
Calories: 132

FRUIT AND YOGURT SHERBET ♡

1 cup unsweetened fruit (peaches, raspberries, or strawberries)
1 ripe banana, sliced
1 cup plain low-fat yogurt
¾ cup unsweetened orange juice
½ cup crushed canned pineapple, packed in unsweetened juice
9 packets (9 grams) EQUAL® Tabletop Sweetener

Drain all fruits, then combine all ingredients in a blender or food processor. Puree until smooth and creamy. Pour into ice cube tray or loaf pan and freeze until firm. Place frozen mixture in large bowl and beat until creamy. Return to freezer container, cover, and freeze until firm, 5-6 hours. Allow to soften slightly before serving.

Garnish with a favorite fruit—a twist of lemon peel, orange slice, or fresh strawberry.

Servings: 6 (½-cup) servings
Exchanges: 1 Bread
Calories: 80

LEMON SHERBET ♡

1 envelope (1 Tbsp.) unflavored gelatin
2 Tbsp. cold water
1½ cups skim milk
½ cup lemon juice
pinch salt
12 packets (12 grams) EQUAL® Tabletop Sweetener
½ tsp. lemon extract
3-4 drops yellow food coloring
1 egg white

Sprinkle the unflavored gelatin over the cold water and wait for gelatin to soften. Heat milk in saucepan until it is steaming but not boiling. Remove milk from heat, add gelatin, and stir to dissolve. Add lemon juice, salt, Equal, lemon extract, and yellow food coloring. Do not worry if the mixture curdles. Bring mixture to room temperature, pour into ice cube tray, and place in freezer for 1 hour. Do not let mixture freeze solid. Beat egg whites until stiff peaks form. Transfer partially frozen mixture to a bowl and beat mixture until fluffy but not melted. Fold in egg whites, pour into covered container, and freeze until firm.

If quantity counts, this recipe is just for you! Garnish with a twist of lemon.

Servings: 4 (1-cup) servings
Exchanges: 1 Fruit
Calories: 48

MINT SHERBET ♡

1 envelope (1 Tbsp.) unflavored gelatin
2 Tbsp. cold water
1½ cups skim milk
12 packets (12 grams) EQUAL® Tabletop Sweetener
½ cup lemon juice
pinch salt
¼ cup creme de menthe
1 egg white

Sprinkle gelatin over cold water and wait for it to soften. Heat milk in saucepan until it is steaming but not boiling. Remove from heat, add gelatin and Equal, and stir to dissolve. Add lemon juice, salt, and creme de menthe. Do not worry if mixture curdles. Pour into ice cube tray and freeze for 1 hour. Do not let mixture freeze solid. Beat egg white until stiff peaks form. Transfer frozen mixture in mixing bowl, and beat mixture until fluffy but not melted. Fold in egg whites, pour into covered container and freeze.

A fresh mint leaf brings out the color and flavor of this dessert. This dessert is delightful after a summertime luncheon. Or try this in a Grasshopper Shake, page 89.

Servings: 8 (½-cup) servings
Exchanges: 1 Fruit
Calories: 38

MIXED FRUIT ICE ♡

1 can (16 oz.) apricots, packed in unsweetened juice
1 can (16 oz.) crushed pineapple, packed in unsweetened juice
12 packets (12 grams) EQUAL® Tabletop Sweetener
3 packages (10 oz.) frozen unsweetened strawberries (or 2 lb. fresh)
1 can (6 oz.) can frozen orange juice concentrate, unsweetened
2 Tbsp. lemon juice
3 bananas, diced

Drain apricots and pineapple. Reserve juice and add water, if necessary, to make 1 cup. Put juice in a large bowl and add Equal, strawberries, orange juice, and lemon juice. Cut up apricots and bananas and add to bowl along with pineapple. Place paper baking cups in muffin tins. (You'll need about 30 paper cups.) Fill cups with mixture and freeze until solid. Remove cups from tins and store them in sealed plastic bags. Take paper cups out of freezer 10-20 minutes before serving.

Make freezer pops for the kids. Place a stick into each muffin tin before freezing the fruit.

Servings: 30
Exchanges: 1 Fruit
Calories: 38

MOCHA TREAT

1 egg white, chilled
1 Tbsp. instant coffee
⅛ tsp. salt
8 packets (8 grams) EQUAL® Tabletop Sweetener, divided
½ cup heavy cream
1 tsp. vanilla extract
⅛ tsp almond extract
½ cup evaporated skim milk
¼ cup chopped almonds

Beat egg white until it is frothy, then add coffee and salt. Continue beating until soft peaks form. Add 3 packets Equal and beat until whites are stiff but not dry. Combine cream, remaining Equal and extracts. Beat until cream is stiff. Fold cream into beaten egg and coffee mixture. Beat chilled evaporated milk until peaks form and fold into coffee mixture. Gently fold in nuts and pour into individual dessert dishes. Freeze until firm.

A must for coffee ice cream lovers! Garnish with a spoonful of whipped topping and a sprinkle of chopped nuts.

Servings: 6
Exchanges: 1 Fruit and 2 Fat
Calories: 119

VANILLA AIR ♡

1 cup instant nonfat dry milk
1 cup ice water
4 Tbsp. lemon juice
5 packets (5 grams) EQUAL® Tabletop Sweetener
1 tsp. vanilla extract

Place dry milk and ice water in mixer bowl. Beat at high speed. When the milk forms soft peaks, add the lemon juice. Continue beating at high speed until stiff peaks form (about 10 minutes). Add Equal and vanilla and beat in well. Pour into plastic freezer container and freeze until firm.

Turn Vanilla Air into Chocolate, Cinnamon, or Coffee Air. To make Chocolate Air, add 1½ tablespoons of cocoa powder in addition to vanilla extract. The mixture will deflate, but this is OK. To make Cinnamon Air, add 1½ teaspoons cinnamon in addition to vanilla. To make Coffee Air, add 1½ teaspoons instant coffee in addition to vanilla. The servings, exchanges, and calories for these variations are the same as for Vanilla Air.

Servings: 4 (1-cup) servings
Exchanges: ¾ Milk
Calories: 61

HINTS TO MAKE YOUR PIES A SUCCESS

You can enjoy the all-American dessert! In this chapter, you'll find a pie recipe for every occasion.

If you can't afford the calories in the pie crust, don't despair! These pie fillings make excellent desserts in their own right—just pour them into pretty dessert dishes and enjoy!

Most of these recipes produce the best results when prepared and served the same day. Because they do not contain sugar, they tend to "weep." Thus, they will be a little watery if stored overnight.

To prepare fresh, delicious pies on a moment's notice, make the crusts in advance and freeze them. When you get a craving for pie, you will be halfway there!

Leftover pie is a great frozen dessert. Simply cover well and freeze, then cut into individual servings.

Be very careful when folding. Slide your spatula across the bottom and up the side of the bowl, then bring the spatula back down into the center of the mixture. Folding is always recommended when you need to combine ingredients lightly.

Many of these pie fillings contain a gelatin mixture. Be sure your gelatin is the consistency of egg whites before you fold it into other ingredients. Gelatin that is firmer than this does not fold well, resulting in rubbery lumps in your pie. If your gelatin has become too thick, all you need to do is reheat it and chill again.

Don't fold still warm gelatin into whipped ingredients such as whipped milk. The heat will deflate these volume-dependent ingredients.

Whipped milk can be prepared from either evaporated skim milk or non-fat dry milk. In most of these recipes, they can be used interchangeably. You may substitute an equal measure of dry milk for evaporated milk. To whip non-fat dry milk, use equal parts of milk and cold water.

For best results when whipping milk remember these points:
- Chill evaporated milk thoroughly before whipping. Place the can in the freezer to shorten the chilling time. Also be sure your beaters and bowl are well chilled too!
- Lemon juice helps stabilize whipped milk. For non-fat dry milk, add 2 tablespoons lemon juice for each ½ cup of milk. For evaporated milk, add 1 tablespoon of lemon juice for each cup of milk.
- Whipped milk is quite delicate and does not hold up long. Do not whip it until needed, and use an extra gentle touch when folding it into other ingredients.

Dry milk and evaporated milk will approximately triple in volume when whipped.

To avoid a rubbery skin on the surface of your pie, gently press plastic wrap on the surface of the pie before you refrigerate it.

APPLE GRAHAM PIE ♡

*microwave only

½ cup margarine
18 packets (18 grams) EQUAL® Tabletop Sweetener, divided
1⅓ cups graham cracker crumbs or 16 (2-inch) squares, crushed
5 cups thinly sliced apples (4 medium apples)
1 tsp. ground cinnamon

Place margarine in large glass mixing bowl. Microwave on high setting for 1 minute, until melted. Add 6 packets Equal and crumbs. Mix well. Press half of mixture firmly and evenly into an 8- or 9-inch pie plate. Place apple slices in a large mixing bowl. (The apple slices should be ⅛- to ¼-inch thick.) Add remaining 12 packets Equal and cinnamon, and mix well. Spoon apples into crumb crust and press down. Cover apples with remaining crumbs to make top crust. Press crumbs down firmly, especially at edges, to prevent the pie from bubbling over. Insert temperature probe in the center of pie and cover it with waxed paper. Set probe temperature to 200 degrees and microwave on high setting. (If your microwave oven doesn't have a probe, microwave for 3-minute intervals and check for doneness.) When pie is done, remove from microwave and let stand 10 minutes covered with wax paper. Remove wax paper so crumb topping will dry and crisp.

Serve warm or cold. Try this with Hot Spiced Tea, (Page 91).

Servings: 8
Exchanges: 1 Bread, ½ Fruit, and 1 Fat
Calories: 142

BANANA BAVARIAN PIE ♡

8- or 9-inch Chocolate Wafer Crust (page 79)
1½ cups mashed bananas, about 3 large bananas
4 Tbsp. lemon juice, divided
⅛ tsp. salt
12 packets (12 grams) EQUAL® Tabletop Sweetener
1 envelope (1 Tbsp.) unflavored gelatin
¾ cup cold water, divided
½ cup instant non-fat dry milk powder
2 egg whites
few drops yellow food coloring

Bake the Chocolate Wafer Crust and set it aside. Mash bananas, add 3 tablespoons of the lemon juice, salt, and Equal. Set aside. Sprinkle gelatin over ¼ cup cold water in the top of a double boiler. Heat until dissolved and take off heat. Place dry milk in mixing bowl. Add ½ cup water and the remaining tablespoon of lemon juice. Beat until stiff peaks form, then set aside. Beat egg whites until foamy. Add dissolved gelatin and continue beating until stiff peaks form. Fold banana mixture into egg whites, then fold in whipped milk. Add food coloring. Pour into prepared crust and refrigerate

Garnish with a few crushed chocolate wafers and banana slices dipped in lemon juice to prevent discoloration.

Servings: 8
Exchanges: 1 Fruit (filling only)
1 Fruit, ½ Bread, and 2 Fat (filling and crust)
Calories: 54 (filling only)
172 (filling and crust)

BANANA CREAM PIE

8- or 9-inch Pastry Crust (page 81)
¼ cup cornstarch
¼ tsp. salt
3 cups skim milk
4 egg yolks, slightly beaten
2 Tbsp. margarine, softened
1 Tbsp. plus 1 tsp. vanilla extract
16 packets (16 grams) EQUAL® Tabletop Sweetener
1 small banana

Bake the Pastry Crust and set it aside. Stir together cornstarch and salt in a medium saucepan. Blend milk and egg yolks; gradually stir into dry mixture. Cook over medium heat, stirring constantly, until mixture thickens. Cook 1 minute longer, stirring constantly. Remove from heat; blend in margarine, vanilla, and Equal. Press plastic wrap onto surface of filling in saucepan and cool to room temperature. Peel and slice banana; arrange banana slices in baked pastry crust. Pour in cooled filling. Chill pie thoroughly, at least 2 hours.

Just before serving, top pie with a dollop (1 tablespoon) of whipped topping if desired.

Servings: 8
Exchanges: 1 Bread and 1 Fat (filling only)
2 Bread and 3 Fat (filling and crust)
Calories: 109 (filling only)
269 (filling and crust)

BLACK BOTTOM PIE ♡

10-inch prepared Chocolate Wafer Crust (page 79)
1½ envelopes (1½ Tbsp.) unflavored gelatin
1½ cups skim milk, divided
1 container (8 oz.) low-fat cottage cheese
1 Tbsp. vanilla extract (or rum flavoring)
18 packets (18 grams) EQUAL® Tabletop Sweetener, divided
6 Tbsp. plain cocoa powder
3 egg whites

Bake the Chocolate Wafer Crust and set it aside. Sprinkle gelatin over ¾ cup of the skim milk in a small saucepan. Soften 1 minute then heat gently and stir until gelatin completely dissolves. Place cottage cheese in a blender or food processor; blend until completely smooth. Add gelatin mixture, remaining milk, and vanilla. Cover and blend smooth, scraping down sides of container occasionally. Remove half of the blended mixture to a mixing bowl and set aside. To the half of the mixture remaining in blender, add 9 packets Equal and the cocoa. Blend thoroughly, scraping down container. Pour chocolate mixture into crust and chill until partially set, about 30 minutes. Beat egg whites until stiff. Gradually beat in remaining Equal, then fold the whites into the vanilla mixture in the bowl. Spoon vanilla and egg white mixture over chocolate layer in crust; chill several hours until completely set.

Garnish with a few chocolate curls. To make the curls, soften a square of wrapped, unsweetened chocolate by warming it between your hands or placing it in a warm oven. Form the curl by running a vegetable peeler over the side of square. Gently transfer the curls to a container and freeze until needed.

Servings: 12
Exchanges: 1 Meat (filling only)
1 Bread, 1 Fat, and 1 Meat (filling and crust)
Calories: 62 (filling only)
180 (filling and crust)

BLIZZARD PIE

8- or 9-inch baked Pastry Crust (page 81)
1 envelope (1 Tbsp.) unflavored gelatin
¼ cup cold water
¼ cup flour
½ tsp. salt
1½ cups skim milk
20 packets (20 grams) EQUAL® Tabletop Sweetener, divided
¾ tsp. vanilla extract
¼ tsp. almond extract
½ cup heavy cream
3 large egg whites (½ cup)
¼ tsp. cream tartar
1¼ cups shredded coconut, divided

Bake the Pastry Crust in advance. Soften gelatin in cold water for 5 minutes. Mix the gelatin mixture, flour, salt, and milk in a small saucepan. Cook over low heat, stirring constantly until mixture boils. Boil one minute longer. Remove from heat and stir in 10 packets Equal. Chill. When the mixture is partially set, beat until smooth. Blend in vanilla and almond extracts. Whip cream until stiff, then gently fold into gelatin mixture. Beat egg whites until frothy and add the cream tartar. Gradually beat in remaining 10 packets of Equal. Continue beating until the whites are stiff. Carefully fold whipped cream mixture into the egg whites. Then fold in 1 cup of the coconut and pile into cooled, baked pastry crust. Sprinkle remaining coconut on top. Chill for 2 hours. Remove from refrigerator 20 minutes before serving. Serve cold.

Garnish this pie with thinly sliced kiwi fruit.

Servings: 8
Exchanges: 1 Milk and 1 Fat (filling)
1 Bread, 1 Milk, and 3 Fat (filling and crust)
Calories: 155 (filling)
315 (filling and crust)

BLUEBERRY TARTS ♡

*microwave only

2 Tbsp. margarine
1 graham cracker square (2-inch), crushed
2 Tbsp. water
1 Tbsp. cornstarch
4 packets (4 greams) EQUAL® Tabletop Sweetener
¼ tsp. cinnamon
1 Tbsp. lemon juice
1 pint unsweetened blueberries, fresh or frozen

Put margarine in a small glass bowl and melt it in the microwave (high setting for 1 minute). Add crumbs and toss. Pat crumb mixture into the bottoms of three custard cups. Put the cups in the microwave, high setting, for 1½ minutes, or until set. Put aside. Combine all remaining ingredients, except blueberries, in a medium glass bowl. Add blueberries and toss to coat. Microwave on high setting for 6 minutes, or until mixture thickens, stirring every 1½ minutes. Cool. Spoon blueberries into the custard cups. Cover and chill before serving.

Top with a tablespoon of non-dairy whipped topping.

Servings: 3
Exchanges: 1½ Fruit, ½ Bread, and ½ Fat
Calories: 110

CHOCOLATE EGGNOG PIE

8- or 9-inch Chocolate Crumb Crust (page 79)
1 envelope (1 Tbsp.) unflavored gelatin
⅓ cup cocoa powder
⅛ tsp. salt
3 egg yolks
1¼ cups skim milk
18 packets (18 grams) EQUAL® Tabletop Sweetener, divided
¾ tsp. rum extract
½ tsp. vanilla extract
¼ tsp. ground nutmeg
3 egg whites
½ cup whipping cream

Bake the Chocolate Crumb Crust and set aside. Mix unflavored gelatin, cocoa, and salt in a medium saucepan. Blend in egg yolks and milk. Mix well and let stand 3 minutes. Stir this mixture over low heat until gelatin dissolves completely and mixture thickens slightly, about 5 minutes. Stir in 12 packets Equal, rum extract, vanilla, and nutmeg. Pour into large bowl and chill, stirring occasionally until mixture mounds slightly when dropped from spoon. Beat egg whites until soft peaks form; gradually add 6 packets Equal and beat until stiff. Fold into gelatin mixture. Whip the cream and fold it into the gelatin mixture. Chill 15 minutes. Pour into prepared crust and chill until firm.

You may garnish with a few chocolate curls. (See instructions at the end of the Black Bottom pie, page 67.)

Servings: 8
Exchanges: ½ Meat and ½ Milk (filling only)
1 Fruit, 1½ Meat, and ½ Milk
(filling and crust)
Calories: 118 (filling only)
258 (filling and crust)

CRANBERRY CHIFFON PIE

    8- or 9-inch Graham Cracker Crust (page 80)
    2 Tbsp. cornstarch
    2 cups Cranberry Juice (page 86)
    1 envelope (1 Tbsp.) unflavored gelatin
    ½ tsp. salt
    3 packets (3 grams) EQUAL® Tabletop Sweetener
    3 egg whites
    1 cup frozen whipped topping, thawed

Bake the Graham Cracker Crust and set it aside. Put cornstarch in a small saucepan and dissolve it in a small amount of cranberry juice. Add remaining juice, gelatin, and salt. Cook and stir over medium heat until mixture thickens and bubbles. Remove from heat and stir in the Equal. Pour cranberry mixture into a bowl. Chill, stirring frequently, until mixture mounds slightly when dropped from a spoon. Beat egg whites until stiff peaks form. Fold in cranberry mixture then whipped topping. Pour into prepared crust. Refrigerate until firm.

Garnish the pie with whipped topping and candied green cherries.

Servings: 8
Exchanges: 1 Fruit (filling only)
1 Bread, 1 Fat, and 1 Fruit (filling and crust)
Calories: 53 (filling only)
173 (filling and crust)

DREAMY CHOCOLATE PIE

10-inch Graham Cracker Crust (page 80)
1 recipe Chocolate Pudding (page 19)
2 packages nondairy whipped topping mix
1 cup cold skim milk
1 tsp. vanilla extract

Prepare pudding as directed but put it in a bowl. Place plastic wrap directly on the surface of the pudding to prevent skin from forming. When the pudding has cooled, prepare the nondairy whipped topping with milk and vanilla according to package directions. Fold the cooled pudding into the whipped topping, then pour into the prepared crust.

Garnish with a few chocolate curls or sprinkle with nuts.

Servings: 12
Exchanges: 1 Bread and 1 Fat (filling only)
2 Bread and 2 Fat (filling and crust)
Calories: 101 (filling only)
221 (filling and crust)

EGGNOG PIE

10-inch Pastry Crust (page 81) or Graham Cracker Crust (page 80)
2 envelopes (2 Tbsp.) unflavored gelatin
½ tsp. salt
4 egg yolks
2 cups skim milk
24 packets (24 grams) EQUAL® Tabletop Sweetener, divided
¾ tsp. rum extract
4 egg whites
¼ plus ⅛ tsp. cream of tartar
¾ cup evaporated milk, chilled
¼ tsp. nutmeg

Mix the gelatin and salt in a small saucepan. Blend egg yolks and milk; stir into gelatin mixture. Cook over medium heat, stirring constantly, until mixture thickens. Take pan off heat and stir in 12 packets of Equal and rum extract. Chill the mixture, stirring occasionally, until it mounds slightly when dropped from a spoon. Beat egg whites and cream of tartar until foamy. Beat in 12 packets Equal, a few packets at a time until whites are stiff. Do not underbeat. Fold gelatin mixture into beaten egg whites. Put evaporated milk in a chilled bowl and beat milk until it is stiff. Fold whipped milk into the gelatin mixture. Pour into baked pastry crust. Sprinkle generously with nutmeg. Chill at least 3 hours or until set.

This pie has 1000 fewer calories than a traditional eggnog pie!

Servings: 12
Exchanges: ½ Milk and ½ Meat (filling only)
½ Milk, ½ Meat, 1 Bread, 1 Fat
(filling and crust)
Calories: 63 (filling)
223 (filling and Pastry Crust)

FRESH PEACH PIE ♡

*microwave too!

8-or 9-inch baked Pastry Crust (page 81)
5 cups sliced fresh peaches
1 Tbsp. lemon juice
3 Tbsp. quick-cooking tapioca
½ tsp. ground coriander or cinnamon
12 packets (12 grams) EQUAL® Tabletop Sweetener

First, bake the crust and set it aside. Then proceed with one of these two methods.

Conventional Method Place sliced peaches in a medium saucepan. Stir in lemon juice. Add tapioca and coriander, stir gently and allow to stand 10 minutes. Cook and stir over medium heat until mixture is bubbly and peaches are tender when pierced. Let cool 1 hour, add the Equal, and spoon into baked pastry crust.

Microwave Method: Place sliced peaches in a glass baking dish. Stir in lemon juice. Combine tapioca and coriander, stir gently into peach slices, and allow peaches to stand about 10 minutes. Microwave on high setting, uncovered, 13 minutes or until mixture is bubbly and peaches are tender when pierced; stir 5 or 6 times while cooking. Let cool about 1 hour; sweeten with Equal and spoon into baked pastry crust.

Garnish with a dollop of whipped topping.

Servings: 6
Exchanges: 2 Fruit (filling only)
1 Bread, 2 Fat, and 2 Fruit (filling and crust)
Calories: 78 (filling only)
238 (filling and crust)

LEMON CHIFFON PIE ♡

8- or 9-inch Pastry Crust (page 81)
1 envelope (1 Tbsp.) unflavored gelatin
18 packets (18 grams) EQUAL® Tabletop Sweetener
5 egg yolks
½ cup water
½ cup lemon juice
1 tsp. grated lemon peel
5 egg whites

Bake crust and set aside. Mix unflavored gelatin with 12 packets Equal in medium saucepan. Beat egg yolks with water and lemon juice and blend into gelatin mixture. Let stand 1 minute. Stir over low heat until gelatin is completely dissolved. Add lemon peel. Pour into large bowl and chill, stirring occasionally, until mixture mounds slightly when dropped from a spoon. Beat egg whites in a medium bowl until soft peaks form. Add remaining 6 packets Equal and beat until whites are stiff. Fold into gelatin mixture. Turn into prepared crust and chill until firm.

Garnish with thinly sliced lemon.

Servings: 8
Exchanges: 1 Meat (filling only)
1 Meat and 1 Bread (filling and crust)
Calories: 51 (filling only)
211 (filling and crust)

REFRIGERATOR PUMPKIN PIE

8- or 9-inch Graham Cracker Crust (page 80)
1 envelope (1 Tbsp.) unflavored gelatin
1 tsp. ground cinnamon
½ tsp. ginger
½ tsp. nutmeg
¼ tsp. salt
2 eggs
1 can (13 oz.) evaporated skim milk
1 can (16 oz.) pumpkin
8 packets (8 grams) EQUAL® Tabletop Sweetener

Mix gelatin, spices, and salt in a medium saucepan. Beat eggs and milk together and pour into dry ingredients. Let stand one minute. Stir over low heat until gelatin is dissolved, about 10 minutes. Blend in pumpkin and Equal. Pour mixture into prepared crust. Chill until firm.

Garnish slices with a spoonful of whipped topping and a sprinkle of nutmeg.

Servings: 8
Exchanges: 1 Milk (filling only)
1 Milk, 1 Bread, and 1 Fat (filling and crust)
Calories: 80 (filling only)
200 (filling and crust)

RUM CHIFFON PIE

8- or 9-inch Graham Cracker Crust (page 80)
1 envelope (1 Tbsp.) unflavored gelatin
¼ cup cold water
3 egg yolks
1½ cup skim milk
⅛ tsp. salt
14 packets (14 grams) EQUAL® Tabletop Sweetener
½ tsp. rum extract
3 egg whites

Bake crust and set aside. Soften gelatin in water, about 5 minutes. Beat egg yolks in a small heavy saucepan. Add milk and salt. Cook and stir over medium heat until mixture coats a spoon. Stir in Equal, gelatin and rum extract. Chill until mixture starts to thicken. Beat egg whites until stiff and fold whites into custard. Pour mixture into the pie crust and refrigerate several hours.

To give the pie an island flavor, sprinkle chopped macadamia nuts on top.

Servings: 8
Exchanges: ½ Milk (filling only)
1 Bread, 1 Fat, and ½ Meat (filling and crust)
Calories: 50 (filling only)
170 (filling and crust)

STRAWBERRY BAVARIAN PIE

10-inch Graham Cracker Crust (page 80)
2 envelopes (2 Tbsp.) unflavored gelatin
½ cup cold water
2 egg yolks
6 packets (6 grams) EQUAL® Tabletop Sweetener
few drops red food coloring (optional)
1 Tbsp. lemon juice
2 cups crushed unsweetened strawberries, fresh or frozen
2 egg whites
¼ cup evaporated skim milk, chilled

Bake crust and set aside. Soften gelatin in cold water. (If you are using frozen berries, defrost and drain the berries and use drained juice instead of water.) Beat together egg yolks and Equal. Add softened gelatin and a few drops of red food coloring if desired. Cook over low heat, stirring frequently until gelatin is dissolved and mixture thickens slightly. Remove from heat and add lemon juice. Chill until mixture mounds when dropped from a spoon; fold in strawberries. Beat egg whites until stiff peaks form and fold into strawberry mixture. Beat chilled evaporated milk until soft peaks form, then fold into strawberry mixture. Pour into prepared pie crust.

Garnish with a whole strawberry or a strawberry fan. (To make strawberry fan, select a large ripe strawberry. Wash, but do not remove green top. Slice thinly from the bottom almost to the top, being careful not to cut through the stem. Fan strawberry and place in the center of the pie.) If you use the filling only, pour it into a pretty mold and garnish the unmolded dessert.

Servings: 12
Exchanges: 1 Fruit (filling only)
1 Bread, 1 Fruit, and 1 Fat (filling and crust)
Calories: 30 (filling only)
Calories: 133 (filling and crust)

PIES

CHOCOLATE CRUMB CRUST ♡

1½ cups vanilla wafers, crushed (approximately 28 wafers)
⅓ cup cocoa powder
6 Tbsp. melted margarine
1 packet (1 gram) EQUAL® Tabletop Sweetener

Combine vanilla wafer crumbs, cocoa, and melted margarine in a medium bowl. Press into an 8- or 9-inch pie pan. Bake at 350 degrees for 8 minutes. Sprinkle Equal over warm crust. Cool.

Servings: 8
Exchange: ½ Bread and 2 Fat
Calories: 140

CHOCOLATE WAFER CRUST ♡

8- or 9-inch crust
24 chocolate wafers
2 Tbsp. margarine
10-inch crust
32 chocolate wafers
3 Tbsp. margarine

Heat oven to 350 degrees. Crush chocolate wafers. Melt margarine and blend with the crushed wafers. Press into pie pan. Bake for 8 minutes. Cool.

Servings: 8 per 8- or 9-inch crust; 12 per 10-inch crust
Exchanges: 1 Bread and 1 Fat per serving of an 8-, 9-, or 10-inch crust
Calories: 118 per serving of an 8-, 9-, or 10-inch crust

GRAHAM CRACKER CRUST ♡

8- or 9-inch crust:
16 graham cracker (2-inch) squares (1⅛ cups)
4 packets (4 grams) EQUAL® Tabletop Sweetener
3 Tbsp. margarine

10-inch crust
20 graham cracker (2-inch) squares (1⅔ cups)
6 packets (6 grams) EQUAL® Tabletop Sweetener
¼ cup margarine

Heat oven to 350 degrees. Crush crackers into fine crumbs. Mix crumbs and margarine. Press mixture firmly and evenly against bottom and side of pie pan. Bake 10 minutes for an 8- or 9-inch crust or 15 minutes for a 10-inch crust. Remove from oven and immediately sprinkle Equal over crust. Cool.

**Sevings: 8 per 8- or 9-inch crust; 12 per 10-inch crust.
Exchanges: 1 Bread and 1 Fat per serving of an 8- or 9-inch crust
Calories: 120 per ⅛ of an 8- or 9-inch crust
120 per ¹/₁₂ of a 10-inch crust**

PASTRY CRUST

8 or 9-inch crust
1 cup flour
¼ tsp. salt
⅓ cup plus 1 Tbsp. vegetable shortening
2-3 Tbsp. cold water

10-inch crust
1⅓ cups flour
¼ tsp. salt
½ cup vegetable shortening
3-4 Tbsp. cold water

Measure flour and salt into bowl. Cut into shortening thoroughly. Sprinkle in water, 1 tablespoon at a time, mixing until all flour is moistened and the sides of bowl are nearly free of dough (an additional 1-2 teaspoons of water can be added if needed.) Gather dough into a ball and flatten it into a round on a lightly floured board. With a floured rollng pin, roll dough into a circle 2 inches larger in diameter than the inverted pie pan. Fold pastry into quarters, transfer to pie plate, and unfold it gently. With scissors, trim the excess dough from the edges, leaving a 1-inch overhang. Fold overhang under, even with the edge of the pan. Flute edges. Prick bottom and sides of crust thoroughly with fork. Bake at 475 degrees for 8-10 minutes.

If possible, hook the fluted edge of the pie pan to prevent shrinking and maintain the shape of the crust.

Servings: 8 per 8- or 9-inch crust; 12 per 10-inch
Exchanges: 1 Bread and 2 Fat per ⅛ of an 8- or 9-inch crust
1 Bread and 2 Fat per 1/12 of a 10-inch crust
Calories: 160 per ⅛ of an 8- or 9-inch crust or 1/12 of a 10-inch crust

HINTS TO MAKE YOUR DRINKABLE DESSERTS A SUCCESS

Sometimes it's more enjoyable to sip your dessert than to eat it. Whether it's 100 degrees in the shade or 30 below, you'll find what you're looking for in this chapter.

Cold drinks look even more enticing in frosted glasses. Just place glasses in freezer at least 30 minutes before serving.

If you're not a daily coffee or tea drinker, your supplies will stay fresh if you store them in your freezer in tightly sealed containers.

Some of these recipes call for orange or lemon rind. You can always have rind on hand if you peel your oranges and lemons as you use them and store the rind in the freezer. You can grate some of your oranges and lemons and keep frozen grated rind as well.

For best results when brewing coffee or tea, start with cold water in the kettle.

Dress up your drinks with decorative ice cubes. Fill ice cube trays half full of water, freeze, then arrange fruit or mint leaves on top. Add more water and freeze again. Strawberries, cherries, blueberries, raspberries, and blackberries look especially good in ice cubes. For crystal-clear cubes, fill your trays with water that has been boiled, then cooled.

Store whole lemons in a tightly sealed jar of water in the refrigerator. They will yield much more juice than when first purchased.

If you submerge a whole lemon in hot water for 15 minutes before squeezing, it will yield almost twice the amount of juice. (Or warm it in your oven for a few minutes before squeezing.)

BANANA SHAKE ♡

1 banana, peeled and sliced
1 packet (1 gram) EQUAL® Tabletop Sweetener
2 cups skim milk
dash nutmeg

Put banana, Equal, and milk in a blender and blend on high setting until banana is liquefied. Pour mixture into glasses and top with a dash of nutmeg.

Serve malt-shop style in a tall glass with a straw.

Servings: 2
Exchanges: 1 Milk and 1 Fruit
Calories: 123

CAFE AU LAIT ♡

2 cups skim milk
2 cups water
1½ Tbsp. instant decafinated coffee
2 packets (2 grams) EQUAL® Tabletop Sweetener
4 Tbsp. nondairy whipped topping (optional)
dash nutmeg

Heat milk and water in a medium saucepan but do not boil. Stir in coffee and Equal until both dissolve. Pour into 4 cups.

Garnish with whipped topping, if desired. Sprinkle each serving with nutmeg.

Servings: 4 (1-cup) servings
Exchanges: ½ Milk
Calories: 50

CAPPUCCINO

2 cups skim milk
4 tsp. unsweetened grated chocolate
4-6 packets (4 to 6 grams) EQUAL® Tabletop Sweetener
2 tsp. instant coffee
4 oz. brandy

Heat milk in a small saucepan. Stir in chocolate and coffee. Pour into mugs. Add EQUAL® Tabletop Sweetener to taste. to

Top with whipped topping and grated unsweetened chocolate.

Servings: 4 (½-cup) servings
Exchanges: ¾ Milk and 2 Fat
Calories: 165

CHOCOLATE NOG

1 egg
2 cups skim milk
2 Tbsp. coacoa powder
½ tsp. vanilla extract
4 packets (4 grams) EQUAL® Tabletop Sweetener

Combine all ingredients in a blender or shaker. Blend briefly on low setting or shake vigorously until nog is smooth. Serve immediately.

Consider this for breakfast as well as for a hearty drink.

Servings: 1
Exchanges: 1 Milk and ½ Meat
Calories: 134

CITRUS BUTTERMILK COOLER ♡

¼ cup unsweetened orange juice
1½ Tbsp. lemon juice
1 cup cold low-fat buttermilk
4 packets (4 grams) EQUAL® Tabletop Sweetener

Put all ingredients in a blender and blend on low setting until cooler is smooth and foamy. Serve at once.

Garnish with a twist of orange or lemon peel.

Servings: 2 (1-cup) servings
Exchanges: ½ Milk
Calories: 58

COCOA ♡

2 heaping tsp. cocoa powder
1 Tbsp. water
1 cup skim milk
5 packets (5 grams) EQUAL® Tabletop Sweetener

Make a paste of cocoa and water in a small saucepan. Add milk and Equal to cocoa paste and stir to blend all ingredients. Heat well but do not boil.

Make the cocoa and water paste before adding the milk to make sure there will be no lumps in the cocoa. This cocoa warms both body and spirit.

Servings: 1
Exchanges: 1 Milk
Calories: 87

CRANBERRY JUICE ♡

1 lb. cranberries, fresh or frozen
6 cups hot water
6 packets (6 grams) EQUAL® Tabletop Sweetener

Put cranberries and water in a large stainless steel or enameled saucepan. Cover and bring to a boil. Boil 7-10 minutes, stirring occasionally, until cranberries split. Strain. Stir Equal into strained juice and chill.

Reserve drained cranberries and add Equal to taste for a delicious, low-calorie cranberry sauce (½ cup is FREE).

Servings: 12 (½-cup) servings
Exchanges: FREE
Calories: 19

NEW YEAR'S EGGNOG

2 egg yolks
¼ tsp. salt
4 cups skim milk
12 packets (12 grams) EQUAL® Tabletop Sweetener, divided
2 egg whites
1 tsp. vanilla extract
1 tsp. brandy or rum extract.
ground nutmeg

Beat egg yolks in a medium saucepan until they are lemon-colored, add salt, and stir in milk. Cook over medium heat, stirring until mixture coats a metal spoon. Add 8 packets Equal and mix well. Chill milk mixture. Beat egg whites until foamy. Gradually add the 4 remaining packets of Equal and beat until whites form soft peaks. Stir chilled milk mixture into egg whites and vanilla and brandy or rum flavoring. Chill.

Pour eggnog into a punch bowl and sprinkle nutmeg on top for a festive touch.

Servings: 5 (1-cup) servings
Exchanges: 1 Bread and ½ Meat
Calories: 124

FRUIT FRAPPE ♡

1 cup skim milk
1 banana
1 orange, peeled and cut in small pieces
1 strips orange rind
2 packets (2 grams) EQUAL® Tabletop Sweetener
⅛ tsp. almond extract
pinch salt

Blend all ingredients in a food processor or at high setting in a blender. When fruits are entirely liquefied, pour mixture into freezer tray. Freeze partially; do not let mixture freeze solid. Remove from freezer and beat until frappe is frothy but not melted. Spoon into 2 parfait glasses. Freeze until frappe is firm. Remove from freezer 20 minutes before seving.

Dress up the frappe with orange pieces on a toothpick or cocktail skewer.

Servings: 2
Exchanges: ½ Milk and 1½ Fruit
Calories: 100

FROZEN FRUIT SLUSH ♡

½ cup lemon juice
1 cup orange juice
3 small bananas, mashed
3 cups cold water
12 packets (12 grams) EQUAL® Tabletop Sweetener
1 cup crushed pineapple, fresh or packed in unsweetened juice

Mix all ingredients and stir until they are well blended. Pour the liquid into 10 plastic or styrofoam cups (about ¾ cup into each). Freeze. Remove from freezer 40 minutes before serving.

Put each cup into a small self-sealing plastic bag to keep fruit fresh tasting. For easy handling, place the cups in a cake pan when you put them in the freezer.

Servings: 10 (¾-cup) servings
Exchanges: 1 Fruit
Calories: 50

GRASSHOPPER SHAKE ♡

1 Cup Mint Sherbet (page 58)
1 cup skim milk

Blend Sherbet and milk together in blender until shake is smooth and thick. Serve immediately.

Top with a fresh mint leaf.

Servings: 2
Exchanges: 1 Milk
Calories: 78

HOT CHOCOLATE EXCELSIOR

2 squares (2 oz.) unsweetened baking chocolate
1 cup water
4 packets (4 grams) EQUAL® Tabletop Sweetener
pinch salt
3 cups skim milk
1 tsp. grated orange rind
¼ tsp. almond extract
¼ tsp. vanilla extract

Melt chocolate in water on top of double boiler, over low heat, stirring constantly. Add salt and orange rind. Then add milk gradually and heat thoroughly, but do not boil. Remove from heat, add Equal, almond and vanilla extracts, and beat until chocolate is frothy. Pour into 6 mugs.

Garnish with a dollop of whipped topping and a twist of orange rind.

Servings: 6 (½-cup) servings
Exchanges: ½ Milk and ½ Fat
Calories: 64

HOT CIDER ♡

½ tsp. whole allspice
½ tsp. whole cloves
1 stick cinnamon
½ cup water
1½ cup Cranberry Juice, unsweetened (page 86)
1 quart apple cider, unsweetened

Combine all ingredients in a large saucepan and simmer 5 minutes. Strain to remove spices.

A cinnamon stick swizzle stick in each mug adds a spicy note.

Servings: 12 (½-cup) servings
Exchanges: 1 Fruit
Calories: 43

HOT SPICED TEA ♡

4 tsp. black tea leaves
2 tsp. whole cloves
10 cups boiling water, divided
½ cup orange juice
1 cup lemon juice
18 (18 grams) EQUAL® Tabletop Sweetener

Place tea leaves and cloves in a teapot or large enameled saucepan. Pour 5 cups boiling water over tea leaves and cloves. Steep 1 hour and strain. Pour tea back into saucepan and add orange juice, lemon juice, Equal, and remaining 5 cups boiling water. Heat through. Serve.

The flavor of this tea improves upon standing, so make it ahead of time and heat individual servings when needed.

Servings: 12 (1-cup) servings
Exchanges: FREE
Calories: 14

LEMONADE ♡

2 lemons, large
1 medium orange
12 packets (12 grams) EQUAL® Tabletop Sweetener
1 quart water

Squeeze lemons and oranges. Add Equal and water and stir well. Serve over ice.

You may garnish with a slice of lemon or orange or with a mint leaf. Serve in a frosted glass for a cool touch.

Servings: 8 (½-cup) servings
Exchanges: FREE per ½-cup serving and 1 Fruit per 1-cup serving
Calories: 32 per 1 cup

ORANGE JULIET ♡

1 cup skim milk
1 cup water
3 packets (3 grams) EQUAL® Tabletop Sweetener
1 tsp. vanilla extract
12 ice cubes
1 can (6 oz.) orange juice concentrate, unsweetened

Put all the ingredients in a blender and blend until the Juliet is smooth and frothy. Serve immediately.

Garnish with a twist of orange. If you do not drink this immediately, put it in the blender again. It will not be as frothy the second time around, however.

Servings: 8 (½-cup) servings
Exchanges: 1 Fruit
Calories: 32

RHUBARB PUNCH ♡

4 cups rhubarb, diced
2 cups water
1 cinnamon stick
10 cloves
24 packets (24 grams) EQUAL® Tabletop Sweetener
1 cup orange juice
½ cup lemon juice
½ cup lime juice
3 cups cold water
1 tsp. vanilla extract

Cook first 4 ingredients over low heat in a medium saucepan, covered, until the rhubarb is tender, about 10 minutes. Strain and press rhubarb to extract juice. Reserve the juice and discard the remaining pulp. Dissolve the Equal in the reserved juice. Cool. Add remaining ingredients and pour into punch bowl with ice.

Try fancy ice cubes (page 83) for a special touch.

Servings: 8 (1-cup) servings
Exchanges: 1 Fruit
Calories: 51

WINTER WARMER

2 cups orange juice, unsweetened
1 cup water
1 cup Cranberry Juice (page 86)
½ cup pineapple juice, unsweetened
1 Tbsp. lemon juice

Combine all ingredients in a large stainless steel or enameled saucepan and heat until boiling. Reduce heat and simmer 5 minutes. Serve hot.

Add a slice of orange or lemon for color and flavor.

Servings: 6 (²⁄₃ cup) servings
Exchanges: 1 fruit
Calories: 44

HINTS TO MAKE YOUR GELATINS A SUCCESS

Dissolve completely before moving on to the next step of your recipe. If gelatin is not dissolved properly, your dessert will not set.

Fresh or frozen pineapple, figs, kiwis, mangos, papayas, and their juices contain an enzyme that prevents gelatin from setting. However, these fruits and juices will work well if they are canned.

Thicken gelatin to the consistency of egg whites before adding solid food, or the food will settle to the bottom and be crowded at the top of the unmolded dessert.

Drain fruits thoroughly and thaw and drain frozen fruits completely before adding them to a gelatin mixture. Poorly drained fruits add excess water to the gelatin and prevent it from setting. You can reserve the drained liquid and substitute it for the liquid the recipe calls for.

Spray the mold with non-stick spray before filling to make unmolding easier.

To unmold a gelatin dish:

- Fill a large bowl or pot (or your kitchen sink) with warm (not boiling) water. Immerse the mold in the water to just below the rim for about 10 seconds. Remove mold from the water and dry outside of the dish.
- Tilt the mold from side to side to ease the gelatin away from the sides and allow air in. If necessary, gently pull the gelatin away from the sides of the mold with your fingertips or a knife.
- Place the serving dish over the mold. Using both hands, invert the mold over the dish.
- If necessary, shake gently or tap around the mold with a spoon.
- If you held your mold in the water too long and it is starting to melt, leave the mold in the dish and return to the freezer for 10 minutes. Repeat unmolding procedure, but this time immerse in hot water for only 5 seconds.

Preformed plastic molds with removable centers are very easy to use. You do not need to immerse these in water; just invert over your serving plate. Pull out the center and ease out the gelatin.

To center your mold on its serving dish easily, rinse the serving dish in cold water before you unmold the gelatin. You will then be able to slide the mold into place.

BLACKBERRY GELATIN MOLD ♡

2 envelopes (2 Tbsp.) unflavored gelatin
2 packets black cherry flavored sugar-free powdered drink mix, sweetened with Nutrasweet™
4 cups water, divided
1 cup chopped fresh or frozen unsweetened blackberries

Mix unflavored gelatin and soft drink mix in a medium bowl. Boil 2 cups water and stir into gelatin mixture until dissolved. Stir in remaining 2 cups cold water. Chill to the consistency of unbeaten egg whites. Gently fold in the blackberries and chill in a 6-cup mold until firm.

Top with a dollop of whipped topping and one blackberry.

Servings: 10 (½-cup) servings
Exchanges: ½ Fruit
Calories: 21

CRANBERRIES AND CREAM GELATIN MOLD ♡

2 cups water, divided
1 package (12 oz.) cranberries, fresh or frozen
18 packets (18 grams) EQUAL® Tabletop Sweetener
1 can (20 oz.) crushed pineapple, drained (reserve juice)
2 envelopes (2 Tbsp.) unflavored gelatin
¼ tsp. nutmeg
¼ tsp. salt
1 tsp. grated lemon peel
3 Tbsp. lemon juice
2 cups plain low-fat yogurt

Bring 1 cup of water to a boil in a stainless steel or enameled saucepan and add cranberries. Return to boil, reduce heat, and simmer gently for 10 minutes, stirring occasionally. Remove from heat. Add Equal and stir thoroughly. Cool to room temperature. Drain pineapple and reserve pineapple juice. Combine pineapple juice, additional 1 cup of water, and gelatin in a 2-quart saucepan.

Heat and stir until gelatin dissolves. Remove from heat and stir in cranberry sauce. Add nutmeg, salt, grated lemon peel, and lemon juice. Refrigerate until mixture thickens to the consistency of raw egg whites. Fold in drained pineapple and yogurt. Spoon into 6-cup mold and chill until firm.

If you can afford the extra fat or would like an alternative to yogurt, replace the yogurt with sour cream, which will add 28 calories per serving.

Servings: 12 (½-cup) servings
Exchanges: 1½ Fruit (with yogurt)
1 fruit + 1 fat (with sour cream)
Calories: 60 (yogurt)
Calories: 88 (sour cream)

FRUIT COCKTAIL GELATIN ♡

2 envelopes (2 Tbsp.) unflavored gelatin
2 packets strawberry or cherry flavored sugar-free powdered drink mix, sweetened with Nutrasweet™
4 cups water, divided
1 cup unsweetened fruit cocktail, drained
1 small banana, sliced

Mix unflavored gelatin and soft drink mix in a medium bowl. Boil 2 cups water and stir into gelatin mixture until dissolved. Stir in remaining 2 cups cold water. Chill to the consistency of unbeaten egg whites. Gently stir in the drained fruit cocktail and sliced banana. Chill until firm in 6-cup mold or individual dessert dishes.

Use a frilly toothpick to make a mini fruit kabob as a garnish for each dessert dish.

Servings: 8 (¾-cup) servings
Exchanges: 1 Fruit
Calories: 36

RASPBERRY BAVARIAN ♡

1 package (10 oz.) frozen unsweetened raspberries, thawed
1 envelope (1 Tbsp.) unflavored gelatin
¼ cup cold water
1 egg white
3 packets (3 grams) EQUAL® Tabletop Sweetener
1 cup plain low-fat yogurt

Drain raspberries and reserve ¾ cup of their juice. (Add water to make ¾ cup if necessary.) In medium saucepan sprinkle gelatin over water until it softens, then stir in raspberries and juice. Heat until gelatin dissolves. Chill gelatin fruit mixture to the consistency of raw egg whites. Beat egg white until frothy and gradually add Equal. Beat until stiff peaks form. Fold beaten white into gelatin mixture. Fold in yogurt and pour into parfait glasses. Chill until set.

This is pretty chilled in a decorative mold.

Servings: 8
Exchanges: 1 Fruit or ½ Milk
Calories: 50

SUGAR-FREE GELATIN ♡

1 envelope (1 Tbsp.) unflavored gelatin
8 packets (8 grams) EQUAL® Tabletop Sweetener
2 cups water, divided
1 packet sugar-free powdered drink mix, any flavor

Mix unflavored gelatin and Equal in a medium bowl. Boil 1 cup water and stir into gelatin until it is completely dissolved. Add the remaining 1 cup cold water. Pour into 2-cup mold or individual dessert dishes and chill until firm.

You can substitute one package sugar-free powdered drink mix presweetened with Nutrasweet™ (aspartame) for the Equal and unsweetened soft drink mix. If the mixture is too sweet for you, use 2 envelopes gelatin and 4 cups water instead of the amounts above. You will get 8 servings and a taste that is not quite so sweet.

If you don't use a mold, make the gelatin in a shallow baking pan. Then cut it into tiny cubes, pile them into parfait glass, and garnish with a perfect morsel of fruit. Try making a variety of colored gelatins for "gelatin jewels."

Servings: 4
Exchanges: FREE
Calories: 16 per ½ cup

ZERO-CALORIE CRANBERRY GELATIN ♡

1½ cups ground fresh cranberries
12 packets (12 grams) EQUAL® Tabletop Sweetener
2 envelopes (2 Tbsp.) unflavored gelatin
¼ tsp. salt
2 cups boiling water
1½ cups cold water
1 Tbsp. lemon juice
¼ tsp. cinnamon
⅛ tsp. cloves
2-3 drops red food coloring
1 orange, sectioned and diced

Combine cranberries and Equal and set aside. Dissolve gelatin and salt in boiling water. Add cold water, lemon juice, cinnamon, cloves, and food coloring. Chill until mixture mounds on a spoon. Fold in cranberries and the orange. Spoon into 4-cup mold. Chill until firm, about 4 hours. Unmold.

Garnish with orange twists. For a holiday touch, garnish with holly.

Servings: 8 (½-cup) servings
Exchanges: Free
Calories: zero

HINTS TO MAKE YOUR ELEGANT DESSERTS A SUCCESS

Impress your guests with a smashing finale to your meal. Enjoy each mouthful while you savor their compliments—the low calories can be your secret.

Remember the old saying, "The eyes eat first." Make sure your dessert presentation brings out the beauty of these dishes:

- Clear the table to set the scene for the elegant dessert to come. Clear previous courses, brush up crumbs, and blot spills and stains. Fresh glassware and clean napkins set the proper mood.
- Pull out all the stops: use your best silver, crystal, and china.
- Be sure the dessert dishes are the appropriate size for the serving. A small portion looks lost in a large dish, and you may be tempted to make the portions too large.

BLUEBERRY ANGEL CAKE

1 cup water
2 cups frozen, unsweetened blueberries, thawed
1 tsp. cornstarch
12 packets (12 grams) EQUAL® Tabletop Sweetener
1 plain angel food cake
½ cup nondairy whipped topping
¼ cup shredded coconut

Mix water and blueberries in saucepan and cook over medium heat until sauce begins to bubble and thicken. Make a smooth paste of cornstarch and 1 teaspoon water and add to blueberry sauce. Stir well. Continue to cook until sauce is thick. Remove from heat, add Equal, and refrigerate. About 1 hour before serving, place cake on a platter and "frost" with chilled blueberry sauce by placing berries on top of cake and in the center and covering the sides with the liquid portion of the sauce. Just before serving, put dollops of whipped topping on the cake and sprinkle with the coconut.

This cake is especially attractive served on a brass or silver platter.

Servings: 10
Exchanges: 1 Bread and 1 Fruit
Calories: 99

CHEESEBERRY CREPES

*microwave only

4 oz. Neufchatel cheese
6 packets (6 grams) EQUAL® Tabletop Sweetener
1 tsp. grated lemon rind
2 Tbsp. lemon juice
10 crepes (page 103)
1 recipe Brandied Blackberry Sauce (page 32) or Cherry Rum Sauce (page 41)

Make a filling by beating cheese with Equal, lemon rind, and lemon juice. Spoon equal amounts into each prepared crepe, roll, and arrange in a glass or baking dish. Microwave on medium heat, rotating dish one quarter turn every minute, until crepes are evenly warmed. Top with chilled sauce.

Garnish with chopped almonds or a twist of lemon rind.

Servings: 5 (2 crepes each)
Exchanges: 1 Meat and 1 Fruit per 1 crepe
1 Meat, 2 Fruit, and 1 Fat per 2 crepes
Calories: 100 per 1 crepe
200 per 2 crepes

DESSERT CREPES

2 eggs
2 tsp. brandy
½ cup flour
¾ cup skim milk
3 packets (3 grams) EQUAL® Tabletop Sweetener
1 tsp. melted margarine

Beat eggs well. Add brandy to the beaten eggs. Sift flour into this mixture, then fold in milk. Add Equal and melted margarine. Beat with an electric mixer until thin, smooth batter is formed. To cook, heat an 8-inch crepe pan or frying pan. (If it does not have a no-stick surface, you may want to spray it with a non-stick cooking spray.) Pour about 2 teaspoons of the batter into the pan, tilting the pan so that the batter covers the bottom of the pan completely. When one side of the crepe is done (about 1 minute) turn the crepe over and cook the other side. The second side will not brown as well as the first and should be on the inside when the crepes are filled and rolled. As the crepes are finished, stack them, separated by pieces of waxed paper or doilies.

Crepes may be made ahead and refrigerated or frozen.

Servings: 10 crepes
Exchanges: 1 Meat and 1 Fruit per 2 crepes
Calories: 101 per 2 crepes

ECLAIRS

½ cup hot water
¼ cup margarine
½ cup flour
¼ tsp. salt
2 eggs
1 recipe Vanilla Pudding (page 28)
1 recipe Fudge Sauce (page 37)

Preheat oven to 425 degrees. In medium saucepan, heat water and margarine to boiling. Stir in flour and salt. Cook over medium heat, stirring constantly until mixture forms smooth ball an no longer adheres top the sides of the pan. Remove from heat. Add eggs one at a time, beating mixture until it is smooth and glossy. Spoon dough to an ungreased cookie sheet to make 12 eclairs. Each eclair should be an oval about 5 inches long and 1 inch wide. Bake at 425 degrees for 30-40 minutes or until golden brown. Cool completely. Split, remove filaments of dough from the cavities, and fill with Vanilla Pudding. Top with Fudge and serve.

For a change, fill the eclairs with fresh fruit and top with Custard Sauce, page 38.

Servings: 12
Exchanges: 1 Fat and ½ Fruit per 1 unfilled eclair
1 Milk and 1 Fat per filled eclair
Calories: 68 per unfilled eclair
139 per filled eclair

LEMON CHEESECAKE

*microwave only

1 package (8 oz.) Neufchatel cheese/low calorie cream cheese
1 Tbsp. fresh lemon juice
1 Tbsp. grated lemon peel
2 eggs
6 packets (6 grams) EQUAL® Tabletop Sweetener
1½ graham cracker squares, crushed

Soften Neufchatel cheese. Add lemon juice, lemon peel, eggs, and Equal. Beat with electric mixer at medium speed for 2 minutes, or until well blended. Pour into 9-x-5 loaf dish. Sprinkle graham cracker crumbs on top. Protect ends of dish with 2-inch strips of foil. Microwave on medium setting (50 percent) 6-10 minutes or until center is set but still soft. Give the dish a quarter turn every 2 minutes as it cooks. Remove cheesecake from oven, bring to room temperature, and chill.

Top with Strawberry Topping,(page 33)or with fresh strawberries.

Servings: 6
Exchanges: 1 Meat and 1 Fat
Calories: 135

've# PEACH CHARLOTTE ♡

1 can (16 oz.) peach halves in unsweetened juice
1 envelope (1 Tbsp.) unflavored gelatin
¼ tsp. salt
2-3 drops almond extract
2 egg whites
6 packets (6 grams) EQUAL® Tabletop Sweetener
red and yellow food coloring
½ cup evaporated skim milk, very cold
8 ladyfingers, plain

Drain peaches and reserve juice. Add water to reserved juice, if necessary, to equal ½ cup. In a small saucepan, combine juice, unflavored gelatin, and salt. Stir over low heat until gelatin is dissolved. Chill mixture until it is the consistency of egg whites. Reserve one peach and dice remainaing peaches. Place gelatin mixture, almond extract, egg whites, and half the diced peaches in a large bowl. Beat with electric mixer until whites are fluffy, about 10 minutes. Mix in the Equal. Add enough food coloring to achieve a soft peach color. Chill in refrigerator until mixture mounds slightly when dropped from a spoon. Whip chilled evaporated milk until stiff peaks form. Fold whipped milk and remaining peaches into partially set gelatin. Line sides of 8-inch springform pan with ladyfingers split lengthwise. Pour in filling. Chill until firm. Remove sides of pan at serving time. Slice remaining peach and garnish the charlotte with the slices.

Remember not to remove the sides of the spring form pan until you are ready to serve. This charlotte is best if made and served on the same day.

Servings: 8
Exchanges: 1 Bread
Calories: 86

ELEGANT DESSERTS

SPANISH CREAM WITH STRAWBERRY SAUCE

2 envelopes (2 Tbsp.) unflavored gelatin
½ cup water
3 cups skim milk
3 egg yolks
18 packets (18 grams) EQUAL® Tabletop Sweetener, divided
1 tsp. vanilla extract
3 egg whites
2 cups fresh strawberries or frozen unsweetened strawberries, thawed

Put cold water in a medium saucepan and sprinkle gelatin over it. Let the gelatin stand 5 minutes. Stir over medium heat until gelatin dissolves. Add milk and cook just until mixture boils. Take off heat, transfer ½ cup of the hot milk mixture to a measuring cup and let it cool briefly. Gradually stir the ½ cup into the egg yolks. Return this to the remaining milk mixture. (The milk mixture cannot be too hot or eggs will begin to curdle and not blend smoothly.) Stir over medium-low heat until mixture coats a metal spoon. Take from heat and add 12 packets of Equal and vanilla. Cool until slightly thicker than unbeaten egg whites. Beat egg whites in a large bowl until stiff peaks form. Fold egg whites into milk mixture until well blended. Pour into 5-cup mold. Cover and chill about 3 hours or until firm. Meanwhile, puree the strawberries in a food processor or blender with the remaining 6 packets of Equal to make a strawberry sauce. Top the unmolded dessert with this sauce.

The Spanish Cream tastes and looks elegant—a Valentine special!

Servings: 10
Exchanges: 1 Meat and ½ Fruit
Calories: 66

108 ELEGANT DESSERTS

TRIFLE

    2 Tbsp. slivered almonds
    1 recipe Vanilla Pudding (page 28)
    ½ cup Strawberry Topping (page 33)
    2 packages (3 oz. each) ladyfingers, plain
    1 package (16 oz.) frozen unsweetened strawberries, thawed
      and drained
    1 envelope nondairy dessert topping mix

Toast almonds and set aside. Prepare Vanilla Pudding and refrigerate in saucepan until cool. While pudding cools, prepare Strawberry Topping and cool. To assemble trifle, first split ladyfingers lengthwise into halves. Spread each half with Strawberry topping. Layer one quarter of ladyfingers (topping side up) in the bottom of a wide serving bowl. Top with half the strawberries, then half the pudding. Repeat. Arrange remaining ladyfingers around the edge of the bowl, gently easing them down into the pudding so that they remain upright. Place them so that the topping-covered side faces the center. Prepare nondairy topping mix according to package directions and frost the top of the trifle with the topping. Sprinkle the toasted almonds on top. Refrigerate until serving time. This dessert is best if made and served on the same day.

You'll get beautiful results when you prepare and serve the trifle in a glass bowl.

Servings: 10
Exchanges: 2 Bread and 1 Fat
Calories: 185

Appendix: Exchange Information

Wouldn't it be nice to not have to count the calories in the foods you eat? Wouldn't life be simple if you merely ate a certain number of foods from each group daily and arrived at your desired calorie intake? This is why the food exchange system was developed by the American Dietetic Association and the American Diabetes Association. The exchange system is a simple way of classifying nutritionally similar foods so that a serving of any item from a given list will give you approximately the same number of calories, carbohydrate, protein, and fat.

A dietitian can help you develop an individualized meal plan. (To find a qualified dietitian, contact your local Dietetic Association, Diabetes Association, or hospital outpatient department.)

HOW TO USE THE EXCHANGE LISTS:

The term *exchange* often seems to give people difficulty. Perhaps a better term would be *choice*. We all choose what we will eat each day. Unfortunately, sometimes those choices are not the best for us. The exchange system helps make sure we receive the right foods.

No two people are exactly alike. Their requirements for the kinds and amounts of foods differ. For this reason it is very important to discuss with your dietitian or physician exactly the proper meal pattern for you. Once this is done, simply selecting the right amounts from each list will provide the requirement.

Since one day is not exactly the same as the next, it is sometimes necessary to have more than one meal pattern. Make sure you come away from your diet counseling session with something you can live with. Diets do no good gathering dust in a drawer.

Although the exchange system was designed for diabetics, it is used by many individuals and groups for weight control and weight maintenance.

There are six groups with the diet. Each group contains food approximately equal in calories, carbohydrates, protein, and fat. In addition each group contains similar minerals and vitamins.

In order to help facilitate use of the exchange system, every effort was made to round off these recipes to the nearest 1/2 exchange.

Occasionally it is necesssary to substitute between exchange groups. This should only be done when absolutely necessary. The following substitutions can be made.

> 1 low fat milk; 80 calories and 12 gm. carbohydrate =
> 1 fruit and 1 fat; 85 calories and 10 gm. carbohydrate or
> 1 bread; 70 calories and 15 gm. carbohydrate.
> 1 bread; 70 calories and 15 gm. carbohydrate =
> 3 vegetables; 75 calories and 15 gm. carbohydrate or
> 1½ fruits; 60 calories and 15 gm. carbohydrate
> 1 fruit = 40 calries and 10 grams carbohydrate =
> 2 vegetables; 50 calories and 10 grams carbohydrates

Most diabetic meal patterns allow for switching of 1 ounce meat and all fat exchanges during the day. This is because the meat exchanges break down slowly to sugar in the blood and the fat exchanges do not affect the blood sugar very much. Please check with your dietitian or physician to see if you may safely do this on your diet. If it is allowed you can "save" the extra 1 ounce meat and extra fats from earlier in the day to allow for a special dinner.

LIST 1—MILK EXCHANGES

One exchange of milk contains 12 grams of carbohydrate, 8 grams of protein, a trace of fat and 80 calories.

Non-Fat Fortified Milk
Skim or non-fat milk .... 1 cup
Powdered (non-fat dry, before
    adding liquid) .... 1/3 cup
Canned, evaporated—skim milk . 1/2 cup
Buttermilk made from skim milk . 1 cup
Yogurt made from skim milk (plain,
    unflavored) .... 1 cup

The following milk products have 1/2 additional fat exchange and contain 100 calories.
> Low-Fat Fortified Milk
> 1% fat fortified milk............. 1 cup
> Canned, evaporated—low-fat milk 1/2 cup

The following milk products have 1 additional fat exchange and contain 125 calories.
> 2% fat fortified milk............. 1 cup
> Yogurt made from 2% fortified milk
> (plain, unflavored)............ 1 cup

The following milk products have 2 additional fat exchanges and contain 170 calories.
> Whole milk.................... 1 cup
> Canned, evaporated whole milk.. 1/2 cup
> Buttermilk made from whole milk 1 cup
> Yogurt made from whole milk
> Yogurt made from whole milk
> (plain, unflavored).............. 1 cup

LIST 2—VEGETABLE EXCHANGES

One exchange of vegetables contains about 5 grams of carbohydrate, 2 grams of protein and 25 calories.

This list shows the kinds of vegetables to use to one vegetable exchange. One exchange is 1/2 cup unless noted otherwise.

*Indicates vegetables which contain negligible calories when eaten raw; "free foods."

Alfalfa sprouts*
Artichoke
Asparagus
Bean sprouts
Beets
Beet greens
Broccoli
Brussels sprouts
Cabbage
Carrots
Cauliflower
Celery

Celery cabbage*
Celery root
Chard*
Chayote
Chicory*
Chinese cabbge
Cilantro* (coriander leaf)
Chives*
Collards
Cucumbers
Dandelion*
Eggplant

Endive*
Escarole*
Green beans
Green pepper
Green onions
Jerusalem artichokes
Kale
Leeks
Lettuce*
Mushrooms*
Mustard greens*
Okra
Onions
Palm heart
Parsley
Poke
Red pepper
Radishes*
Rhubarb
Romaine lettuce*
Rutabaga
Sauerkraut
Soybeans
Spinach*
Summer squash
Tomatoes
Tomato juice
Tomato paste (2 Tablespoons)
Tomato sauce (1/4 cup)
Turnips
Turnip greens
Vegetable juice cocktail
Waterchestnuts (5)
Watercress*
Wax beans
Zucchini*

Starchy vegetables are found in the Bread Exchange List.

LIST 3—FRUIT EXCHANGES

One exchange of fruit contains 10 grams of carbohydrate and 40 calories.

Use fresh or packed without sugar unless otherwise specified.

This list shows the kinds and amounts of fruit to use for one fruit exchange.

Apple	1 small
Apple juice or cider	1/3 cup
Applesauce (unsweetened)	1/2 cup
Apricots, fresh	2 medium
Apricots, dried	4 halves
Apricot nectar (sweetened juice)	1/3 cup
Banana	1/2 small
Blackberries	1/2 cup
Blueberries	1/2 cup
Cantaloupe	1/4 small

Cherries	10
Cranberries	Unlimited
Cranberry juice (sweetened)	1/4 cup
Cranberry juice (low calorie)	3/4 cup
Cranberry juice (unsweetened)	Unlimited
Crenshaw melon	2" wedge
Currants	2 Tablespoons
Dates	2
EQUAL®	10 packets
Figs, fresh	1
Figs, dried	1
Fructose	1 Tablespoon
Grapefruit	1/2
Grapefruit juice	1/2 cup
Grapes	12
Grape juice	1/4 cup
Guava	2/3
Honeydew melon	1/8 medium
Kiwi	1
Kumquats, fresh	2
Lemon juice	1/2 cup
Lime juice	1/2 cup
Loquats	3
Lichee	6
Mango	1/2 small
Nectarine	1 small
Orange	1 small
Orange juice	1/2 cup
Papaya	3/4 cup
Passion fruit	1
Passion fruit juice	1/3 cup
Peach	1 medium
Peach nectar (sweetened)	1/3 cup
Pear	1 small
Pear nectar (sweetened)	1/3 cup
Persimmon, native	1 medium
Pineapple	1/2 cup
Pineapple juice	1/3 cup

Plantain .... 1/2 small
Plums .... 2 medium
Pomegranate .... 1 small
Prunes .... 2 small
Prune juice .... 1/4 cup
Raisins .... 2 Tablespoons
Raspberries .... 1/2 cup
Strawberries .... 3/4 cup
Tangerine .... 1 medium
Watermelon .... 1 cup

LIST 4 — BREAD EXCHANGES
(includes Breads, Cereals, and Starchy Vegetables)

One exchange of bread contains 15 grams of carbohydrate, 2 grams of protein, and 70 calories.

Bread:

White (including French and Italian) .... 1 slice
Whole wheat .... 1 slice
Rye or pumpernickel .... 1 slice
Raisin .... 1 slice
Bagel, small 1/2
English muffin, small 1/2
Plain roll, bread 1
Frankfurter roll 1/2
Hamburger bun 1/2
Dried bread crumbs .... 3 Tablespoons
Tortilla, 6-inch 1
Sour dough bread.............. 1 slice
Croutons .... 1/2 cup
Holland rusk .... 2 average
Popover .... 1 average
Bread Sticks (thin) .... 4 (9 inches long)

Cereal:

All bran .... 1/3 cup
Bran flakes .... 1/2 cup
Other ready-to-eat unsweetened cereal .... 3/4 cup

	Puffed cereal (unfrosted)	1 cup
	Cereal (cooked)	1/2 cup
	Grits (cooked)	1/2 cup
	Grape nuts	3 Tablespoons
	Shredded wheat	1 large biscuit
	Wheat germ	1/4 cup
	Matzo farfel	7 Tablespoons
	Corn	1/3 cup
	Corn-on-the-cob	1 small
	Lima beans	1/2 cup
	Parsnips	2/3 cup
	Peas, green (canned or frozen)	1/2 cup
	Potato, white	1 small
	Potato (mashed)	1/2 cup
	Pumpkin	3/4 cup
	Winter squash, acorn, or butternut	1/2 cup
	Yam or sweet potato	1/4 cup
	Chick peas or garbanzo beans	1/4 cup
	Dried beans, peas, lentils (cooked)	1/2 cup
	Baked beans, no pork (canned)	1/4 cup
	Rice, brown (cooked)	1/3 cup
	Rice, white (cooked)	1/2 cup
	Barley (cooked)	1/2 cup
	Wild rice (cooked)	3 Tablespoons
Flours:		
	Arrowroot	2 Tablespoons
	All purpose	3 1/2 Tablespoons
	Bran, unprocessed	5 Tablespoons
	Cake	2 1/2 Tablespoons
	Cornmeal	2 Tablespoons
	Cornstarch	2 Tablespoons
	Matzo meal	3 Tablespoons
	Rye	4 Tablespoons
	Whole wheat	3 Tablespoons
	Bulgur	1 1/2 Tablespoons
	Potato flour	2 1/2 Tablespoons
	Noodles	1/2 cup
	Spaghetti	1/2 cup
	Macaroni	1/2 cup

Crackers:
- Arrowroot 3
- Graham, 2 1/2-inch 2
- Matzo, 4-×-6 inches 1/2
- Oyster........................ 20
- Pretzels, 3 1/8 inches long × 1/8 inch dia. 25
- Rye Wafers, 2-×-3 1/2-inches 3
- Saltines....................... 6
- Soda, 2 1/2-inch square 4
- Pilot crackers 1
- Waverly wafers 6
- Crackers, crushed .... 1/4 cup
- Cracker meal, coarse........... 1/3 cup
- Graham cracker crumbs .... 3 Tablespoons
- Zwieback 3
- Lorna Doone shortbread........ 3
- Vanilla wafers 5

Miscellaneous:
- Cocktail sauce................. 4 Tablespoons
- Popcorn (popped, no fat added) 3 cups
- Tapioca, granulated .... 2 Tablespoons

The following contain 1 additional Fat exchange and a total of 115 calories.
- Biscuit, 2-inch dia.* 1
- Corn bread, 2-inch square, 1-inch thick* 1
- Corn muffin, 2-inch dia. 1
- Crackers, round, butter type* ... 5
- Muffin, plain small*............ 1
- Potatoes, french fried, 2 to 3 1/2 inches 8
- Pancake, 5-×-1/2 inches......... 1
- Waffle, 5-×-1/2 inches........... 1

The following contain 2 additional Fat exchanges and a total of 160 calories.
- Potato or corn chips* 15
- Ice Cream** .... 1/2 cup

* Cholesterol content will depend on type of fat used.
** High cholesterol item

LIST 5—MEAT EXCHANGES

The exchanges in this book do not specify meat exchanges by type. Assume that 1 Meat exchange is a Medium-Fat Meat exchange. The three types of exchanges are given for your information. One exchange of lean meat (1 oz.) contains 7 grams of protein, 3 grams of fat, and 55 calories.

This list shows the kinds and amounts of lean meat and other protein-rich foods to use for one low-fat meat exchange.

Beef: Baby Beef (very lean), Chipped Beef, Chuck, Flank Steak, Tenderloin, Plate Ribs, Plate Skirt Steak, Round (bottom, top), All cuts Rump, Spare Ribs, Tripe .... 1 oz.

Lamb: Leg, Rib, Sirloin, Loin (roast and chops), Shank, Shoulder .... 1 oz.

Pork: Leg (whole rump, center shank), Ham, smoked (center slices) .... 1 oz.

Veal: Leg, Loin, Rib, Shank, Shoulder, Cutlets .... 1 oz.

Poultry: .Meat without skin of Chicken, Turkey, Cornish Hen, guinea Hen, Pheasant .... 1 oz.

Fish: Any fresh or frozen .... 1 oz.
Canned Salmon, Tuna, Mackerel, Crab, and Lobster .... 1/4 cup
Clams, Oysters, Scallops, Shrimp 5 or 1 oz.
Sardines, drained 3
Cheeses containing less than 5% butterfat .... 1 oz.
Cottage Cheese, dry and 2% butterfat .... 1/4 cup
Cheese: Mozzarella, Ricotta, Farmer's cheese, Neufchatel/low calorie cream cheese 1 oz.
Egg (high in cholesterol) 1

	Peanut Butter (This has 2 additional fat exchanges and a total of 168 calories)	2 Tablespoons
	Parmesan (over 5% butterfat)	3 Tablespoons

One exchange high-fat meat (1 oz.) contains 7 grams of protein, 8 grams of fat, and 100 calories.

This list shows the kinds and amounts of high-fat meat and other protein-rich foods to use for one high-fat meat exchange. All items on this list are high in cholesterol.

Beef:	Brisket, Corned Beef (brisket), Ground Beef (more than 20% fat), Hamburger (commercial), Chuck (ground commercial), Roasts (Rib), Steaks (Club and Rib)	1 oz.
Lamb:	Breast	1 oz.
Pork:	Spare Ribs, Loin (Back Ribs), Pork (ground), Country Style Ham, Deviveled Ham	1 oz.
Veal:	Breast	1 oz.
Poultry:	Capon, Duck (domestic), Goose	1 oz.
Cheese:	Cheddar Types	1 oz.
	Cold Cuts	4 1/2-x-1/8-inch slice
	Frankfurter	1 small
	Sausage	1 oz.

LIST 6—FAT EXCHANGES

One exchange of Fat contains 5 grams of fat and 45 calories. # indicates high cholesterol item.

Avocado (4 inches in diameter)	1/8
Bacon fat #	1 teaspoon
Bacon, crisp #	1 strip
Butter #	1 teaspoon
Butter, whipped #	2 teaspoons
Cream, light #	2 Tablespoons
Cream, sour #	2 Tablespoons
1/2 & 1/2, sour #	3 Tablespoons
Cream, heavy #	1 Tablespoon
Cream, whipped, heavy #	2 Tablespoons

Cream cheese # .... 1 Tablespoon
Lard # .... 1 teaspoon
Nuts
- Almonds .... 6 nuts
- Brazil nuts .... 2 medium
- Cashew 3-4
- Filberts 5
- Macadamia .... 4 halves
- Mixed 4-6
- Peanuts, Virginia 10
- Peanuts, Spanish 20
- Pecans .... 2 large whole
- Pistachio 20
- Sunflower seeds .... 1 1/2 Tablespoon
- Sunflower kernels .... 1 Tablespoon
- Walnuts .... 6 small
- Sesame seeds .... 1 Tablespoon

Margarine, regular stick# .... 1 teaspoon
Margarine, soft, tub or stick* .... 1 teaspoon
Margarine, diet .... 2 teaspoons
Oil, corn, cottonseed, safflower, soy,
   sunflower .... 1 teaspoon
Oil, olive .... 1 teaspoon
Oil, peanut .... 1 teaspoon
Olives .... 5 small
Salad dressings**
- Blue Cheese .... 2 teaspoons
- French .... 1 Tablespoon
- Italian .... 1 Tablespoon
- Mayonnaise .... 1 teaspoon
- Salad dressing, mayonnaise type ..... 2 teaspoons

Salt pork .... 3/4-inch cubs

 * Made with corn, cottonseed, safflower, soy, or sunflower oil only.

** If made with corn, cottonseed, safflower, soy, or sunflower oil can be used on fat-modified diet.

Free foods are 20 calories or less per serving. They are not altered in any way; such as sugar being omitted or replaced. Some seasonings and beverages (coffee and tea) are allowed freely because they cannot actually be considered as food, since they provide no nourishment.

SEASONINGS

- Allspice
- Angostura bitters
- Anise
- Basil
- Bay Leaf
- Caraway
- Cardamom
- Celery salt or seed
- Chervil
- Chili powder
- Chives
- Cinnamon
- Cloves
- Cocoa powder—limit 2 teaspoons
- Cumin
- Curry
- Extracts, vanilla, etc.
- Garlic, whole, salt or powder
- Horseradish
- Lemon or orange rind
- Lemon or lime juice— limit to 2 tsp. a day
- Mace
- Marjoram
- Mint
- Mustard, dry or prepared
- Nutmeg
- Onion Salt or Powder
- Oregano
- Paprika
- Parsley
- Pepper
- Pepper, Cayenne
- Poppy Seed
- Poultry Seasoning
- Rosemary
- Saffron
- Sage
- Salt
- Tenderizers
- Thyme
- Vinegar

MISCELLANEOUS:

- Non-stick spray
- Sour pickles
- Some pickle relish
- Dill pickles or other unsweetened pickles
- Cranberries (unsweetened)
- Low-calorie salad dressings (no more than 20 calories per serving)
- Nondairy whipped topping (1 Tablespoon)

BEVERAGES:
Coffee; regular or decafinated
Tea; regular or decafinated
Sanka
Sugar-free pop
Powdered soft drink mix with no sugar added.

SOUPS:
Consomme (without fat)
Bouillon (without fat)
Clear broth
Soups/broth made with foods on this list.

SAUCES:
A-1 Sauce
Catsup (limit to 1 Tablespoon)
Chili sauce (limit to 1 Tablespoon)
Tabasco sauce
Worcestershire sauce (limit to 1 Tablespoon)